Warrior • 11

English Longbowman 1330–1515

Clive Bartlett · Illustrated by Gerry Embleton

First published in Great Britain in 1995 by Osprey Publishing,
Midland House. West Way. Botley. Oxford OX2 0PH, UK
44-02 23rd St, Suite 219, Long Island City, NY 11101, USA
Email: info@ospreypublishing.com

ISBN: 978 1 85532 491 6

CIP Data for this publication is available from the British Library

Military Editor: Iain MacGregor
Design: Alan Hamp

Printed in China through World Print Ltd.

10 11 12 13 14 22 21 20 19 18 17 16 15

FOR A CATALOGUE OF ALL BOOKS PUBLISHED BY OSPREY MILITARY
AND AVIATION PLEASE CONTACT:

Osprey Direct, c/o Random House Distribution Center,
400 Hahn Road, Westminster, MD 21157
E-mail: uscustomerservice@ospreypublishing.com

Osprey Direct, The Book Service Ltd, Distribution Centre,
Colchester Road, Frating Green, Colchester, Essex, CO7 7DW
E-mail: customerservice@ospreypublishing.com

www.ospreypublishing.com

Artist's note

Readers may care to note the original paintings from which the colour
plates in this book were prepared are available for private sale. All
reproduction copyright whatsoever is retained by the Publisher.

For more information visit
www.gerryembleton.com

The Publishers regret that they can enter into no correspondence
upon this matter.

ENGLISH LONGBOWMAN 1330-1515

INTRODUCTION

The period covered by this text has been chosen for two reasons. Firstly, and simply, because it was the great age of English archery. Secondly, because the method of raising the armies differed from that before and after. The end of the 13th century and the beginning of the 14th had been a period of experimentation and development which, by the 1330s, established the 'identity' of the army for the next two hundred years. From the early 16th century the centralisation and increasing authoritarianism of Royal government, coupled with the problems of obtaining sufficient manpower for the ever growing size of armies, a problem exacerbated by a series of historically less well documented, but still vicious, plagues, decreased the military power and influence of the aristocracy and led to the inclusion of substantial numbers of foreign mercenaries. This dearth of native bowmen and use of mercenaries also accelerated the introduction of firearms and subsequent demise of the bow. While this early Tudor period has been considered a time of modernisation of the English army it was also the start of a military decline that lasted for some 125 years.

It would perhaps be more accurate for the title to read 'Archers of the English armies 1330-1515' for these armies usually included considerable numbers of Welshmen and, what may be something of a surprise, some numbers of Frenchmen. It is often overlooked that England owned large areas of France legitimately, through inheritance and marriage. It was a dispute between Edward III of England and Philip VI of France over feudal overlordship that was the root cause of the Hundred Years War, though this war should not be looked upon as continuous. There were two distinct phases, what can be called the 'first French war' of 1337-1380 was always planned as a series of great raids of plunder and

Civilian archers at practice in the 1330s. The 'butts' shown here (distance not to scale!) were constructed of earth and turf and these have a simple white circlet, a 'garland', made of some material for the target. (*The 'Luttrell Psalter'*. British Library Add MS 42130 f147v)

destruction (*chevauchees*) by the English to keep the French occupied and ensure the sovereignty of the English possessions, whereas the 'second French war' of 1415-1453 began as one of planned conquest. Those Frenchmen who were part of the Plantagenet empire, particularly the Gascons, fought alongside their English allies and a few, like the Captal de Buch, achieved great fame. The annexation of Aquitaine by the French in 1453 was decidedly not welcomed by its inhabitants. Similarly, muster rolls and garrison lists from Normandy after the English conquest includes French names among the archers and men-at-arms and many must have faced a difficult choice after French liberation in 1450.

Unfortunately, over the entire period no Englishman thought it necessary to write a treatise on archery. The first such work was penned in 1544 but by a scholar, Roger Ascham, not a soldier. It was not until 1590 that a soldier, one John Smythe, wrote a book discussing military archery, put forward as an argument against the official removal of the bow from the army's weapons list. As with literature, so with illustrations. There are numerous contemporary illustrations of archers but practically every one of them done by a foreign artist or in a foreign workshop. Only in the Luttrell Psalter and the Beauchamp Pageant are there English depictions of comparable quality, though in the Beauchamp Pageant we have perhaps the most accurately observed of them all. As with literature and illustrations, so with artifacts. Until the excavation of the *Mary Rose*, the Tudor warship that sank in 1545, the only surviving examples of medieval archery equipment were a handful of bows, most of dubious authenticity, and a single arrow found in Westminster Abbey in 1878. But despite it being some eighteen years since the first *Mary Rose* artifacts were raised, we still await detailed reports of the, at least, 138 bows and 2,500 arrows recovered and can only draw upon one or two detailed archeological drawings, a few observations written by privileged visitors and what can be gleaned from the exhibits on display. In consequence of all the above, the author hopes he will be forgiven for the number of 'apparently', 'appears to' and 'could be' contained in the text. Fortunately, the author has at least been lucky enough to have been associated with some highly skilled bowyers and fletchers, notably Richard Galloway, and groups of, albeit amateur, practical archeologists. Much of the practical information in the text comes from the research done by these groups.

RECRUITMENT

Until the 17th. century there was no such thing as a standing army in England. Consequently, the campaigns of the 14th and 15th centuries saw the raising of temporary armies which were disbanded on completion of operations. An archer served in one of these armies by either having been conscripted into the 'levy', raised by 'Commission of Array' or recruited into a 'retinue', great or small, of a member of the nobility or gentry in a force raised by 'Contract of Indenture'.

The Hundred Year' war

● English bases in 1380

acquired for Burgundy 1363 -1404

acquired for Burgundy 1419 - 67

Sluy's 1340

BRABANT

Calais Bruges

Agincourt Brussels

1415

LUXEMBOURG

Cherbourg

St. Vaast Harfleur Crécy 1346

Caen

Poissy Paris

Chartres Seine

BRITTANY

Rennes

FRANCE

Nantes

Loire

Orléans

Rumorantin (territory of Valois Kings)

Châlon

Poitiers 1356

Bordeaux Libourne

Périgueur

Lyons

English domains 1339 1360

Dordogne English domains after Peace of Brétigny 1360

Le Puy DAUPHINÉ

Bayonne

Agen

Rhône

Toulouse

Carcassonne

Narbonne

Mediterranean Sea

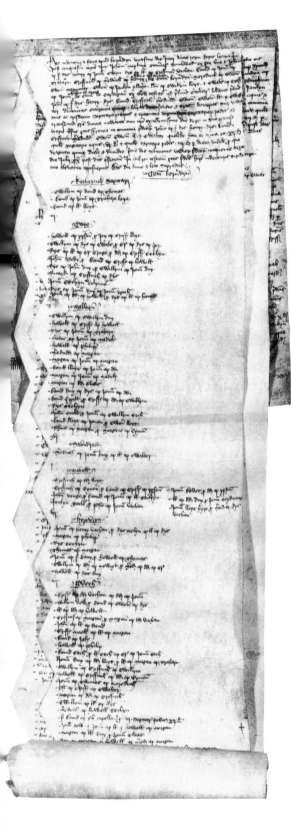

The Commission of Array

The Commission of Array was a legacy of the feudal obligation whereby every man between the ages of 16 and 60 (the posse comitatus) was to serve his county in time of need. This blanket obligation was refined so that 'a selected force of the county was supported by the rest.'[1] According to the Statute of Winchester of 1258, in force until 1558, those with lands or rents worth £2 to £5 a year were, to serve as, (or later to serve as or 'find' i.e. provide), an archer. Counties were assessed as to the number of men they were to supply and 'arrayers', men of considerable standing and appointed under Royal authority, toured their respective counties selecting from the manpower assembled at various designated muster points. They were to choose 'whole and hable' men and had to test every archer listed on the roll. They were also to supply clothing and equipment, and sometimes horses, to pay the men (or give the money to the assigned captain) and either send them to a further muster point or hold them in readiness.

For the unwilling conscript it was possible, particularly after 1343, to escape service by paying a fine, though this was not always accepted. Corruption was not unknown, especially when called upon for the unpopular Scottish campaigns, but nothing like as serious as during the 16th century. It is highly unlikely that an assessed archer could afford to bribe someone of the status of an arrayer but local officials, who were responsible for the mustering of the men and who drew up the roll of names, were occasionally 'encouraged' to remove or change a name on the roll or, having assembled good men before the arrayers, to substitute poor ones after they had left. On the other side of the coin, there would have been volunteers, especially for the French campaigns of the 14th century when the pulpits of the local church gave news of the great victories won and returning soldiers laden with booty showed the material gains possible. Cities also supplied archers under the Array system, usually by the Mayor and Aldermen 'finding' men, and often permitted self-assessment regarding the number to be raised. For example, the City of York's offer of 120 mounted archers for the Scottish campaigns of 1480-81 was accepted by the King, but when called upon again in 1482 the city successfully appealed for a reduction to 100 mounted archers because of the financial burden of its past contribution. Counties were also allowed to appeal if they felt their assessment was too high. During the sporadic civil 'Wars of the Roses', 1455-87, the levy was sometimes in the difficult position of being called out by both

1 M. Powicke, *Military Obligation in Medieval England.*

Looting 14th-century style. Many of the soldiers are wearing the padded gambesons – and note the helmets of laminated construction. (British Library. Royal MS 20 C VII f41v)

claimants to the throne. However, the strength of the feudal tie ensured that they invariably served on whichever side their local lord's or city's allegiance lay.

The Contract of Indenture

The Contract of Indenture, instigated by Edward I at the end of the 13th century, eventually superseded for the nobility their obligatory 40 days feudal service and was simply the adaptation of an existing arrangement used by them to establish a part of their own personal following. Contracts were drawn up between the King and his chief commanders which stipulated the size of the army required, its purpose and the terms and length of service. Depending on the numbers needed, the commander would supplement the men of his own 'indentured retinue' by sub-contracting with members of the nobility and gentry who had their own retainers which, at the lowest level, might consist of only a single man-at-arms (the contractor himself) accompanied by two or three archers. If the King was to lead the expedition he would bring his own retinue as well. To ensure 'fair play' the Contracts, written on parchment, were often duplicated on one sheet which was torn or cut in two to leave each half with a matching serrated edge which were both countersealed. An indentured retinue would consist of any or all of three types of the following personnel: '...first, resident household attendants; secondly, men who are bound by written indenture to serve their lord for life in peace and war; and thirdly, those whose attachment to the lord is shown simply by the acceptance of his fees and the wearing of his badge and livery ...'. [2] An indentured archer could be any one of those three classifications. The household archer was considered an elite, Warwick the Kingmaker once commenting that they were worth two ordinary archers – even English ones. The apex of this class were the King's 'Yeomen of the Crown' who, according to the household regulations of Edward IV (the 'Black Book'), were to be '... most semely persons, clenely and strongest archers... ' and were selected by being '... chosen and tryed out of every lordes house in Ynglond'. The 'domestically' indentured retainer, who signed the same type of contract as the military one, came from the tenantry and neighbourhood of his lord's estates and, though not as good an archer, only really differed from his household counterpart by the fact of not being a permanent resident, otherwise he was usually required to perform many of the same duties and, in return, received many of the same benefits.

The hired retainer was, basically, an itinerant soldier. Some might serve in a retinue for a considerable time, especially those in garrisons in France. It is

2 N. B. Lewis *Indentured Retinues in Fourteenth Century England*

perhaps unfair to judge them purely as mercenaries but these soldiers were almost always temporarily employed and it is they who often resorted to banditry when 'gainful' employment could not be found (ie. after the Treaty of Bretigny in 1360 and the English eviction from Normandy in 1450) and against whom civil complaints about lawlessness are usually directed. Nevertheless, they were professional soldiers and would be archers of great skill. In addition to the above, the King or commander could also employ companies of archers through direct contract. Lastly, mention should be made of the criminals serving in exchange for a 'Charter of Pardon'. This arrangement was quite prevalent during the 14th century (e.g. the company of 200 serving in the Scottish campaign of the winter of 1334-5). Indeed, it has been stated that: 'It seems probable that from two to twelve per cent of most of the armies of the period consisted of outlaws'.[3] The Charters could only be granted by the King and in nearly all cases were given *after* the service had been performed and witnessed. Other conditions were also often stipulated as security but wages were paid at normal rates.

The Levy

In the 14th century Commissions of Array and Contracts of Indenture were used in combination to raise armies for service in Wales, Scotland, Flanders and France but complaints were made by Parliament, the cities and the counties about the legality of some of the terms of service and the continuing costs of the arrayed levy. After a series of legalistic bargainings between a succession of kings and parliaments it was finally re-affirmed that soldiers raised under Commissions of Array would only serve 'domestically' – though, importantly, a concession was granted by Parliament that this included service in Scotland and Wales. Consequently, throughout the 15th century *every* army that left England to serve abroad was raised entirely by Contracts of Indenture. However, it should be noted that the system of Commission of Array extended in the 15th century to captured French lands and any English 'colonist' or Frenchman who held lands or fees by English authority was obliged to serve as a levied soldier when called upon by the King or the King's Lieutenant, as in 1429 when it was ordered that '…all men-at-arms and bowmen…holding fiefs and arriere fiefs… as well English as Normans…' were to assemble at Rouen to join the Duke of Bedford in his defence of Paris. Additionally, because Calais was an English possession populated

An early soldier's pass. It reads: 'Know all that we, the Prince of Wales, have given leave, on the day of the date of this instrument, to William Jauderel, one of our archers, to go to England. In witness of this we have caused our seal to be placed on this bill. Given at Bordeaux, 16th December in the year of Grace 1355'. (Courtesy of the Mostyn-Owen-Jodrell family and the John Rylands Library, Manchester)

3 H.J. Hewitt, *The Organisation of War under Edward III*

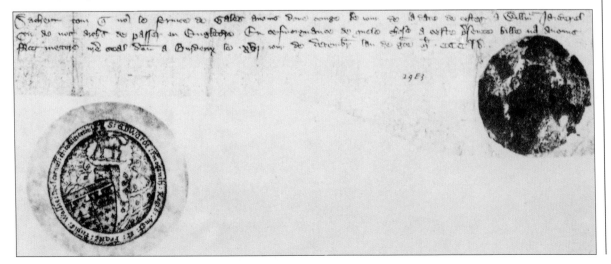

almost exclusively by Englishmen (the indigenous population having been evicted at its capture in 1347) and considered as much a part of England as, say, the Isle of Wight, it was quite legal for levied troops raised at an English Array to be posted there.

The most noticeable difference in the 15th century between an army raised for overseas service and one raised for domestic service was in their respective sizes. As an illustration, for the 1475 French expedition the combined indentured contingents contracted for by the brothers Lord Thomas and Sir William Stanley totalled 42 men-at-arms and 320 archers, but for Henry Tudor's invasion of England in 1485 they mustered some 3,000 household and retained men. Other notable families, such as Percy and Howard, could raise as large, or larger, 'private armies' and if one includes levied troops raised from the whole country it is apparent that in England very large armies could be assembled. Though it is worth adding that contemporary accounts relate how the quality of household and retained men was always of greater value than the simple quantity of the levy.

SERVICE

Not every levied archer was mobilised to serve in a field force. The duty of arrayed archers north of the River Trent was to remain on 'standby' ready to repel any Scottish incursions, particularly likely when the King of England was in France. The most famous example of this being Flodden in 1513. Similarly, men of the coastal counties, especially those facing the English Channel, who lived within a six-league margin of the shore were arrayed and placed on 'standby' to serve in the *'Garde de la Mer'*. Their role was purely to defend their areas against, and repel, any invasion. During the 14th century both they and the men north of the Trent were classified as exempt from service overseas. These 'home defence' levies were stiffened by designated members of the nobility with their retainers. In 1415 Henry V entrusted the Earl of Westmoreland and the lords Mauley and Dacre with 200 lances (i.e. men-at-arms) and 400 archers to guard the East and West Marches facing Scotland, a further 100 lances and 200 archers were allocated to north and south Wales, 150 lances and 300 archers to Calais and 150 lances and 300 archers 'for the sea'. The indenture system was also used to garrison castles and strongholds on the borders and coasts of England and between English- and French-held territory in France. The King either signed contracts with the lord in whose domain the fortification lay, or directly with the castle captain. These contracts were identical to those raised for field forces, agreeing the number of men and the payment terms. They often contained a clause stating that if a garrison came under siege the King was obliged to relieve them within a given time; if that time elapsed the captain was free to make his own terms with the besiegers or simply abandon the position.

Of course, not all English archers served English masters. Many sought employment elsewhere, the best example being those who joined Charles the Bold of Burgundy's army in the 1470s, the majority enlisting after the bloodless French expedition of 1475 when Charles remarked that they might as well fight for him as go back to England and kill each other.

Looting 15th-century style. The clothing and general appearance of these soldiers differs completely from those of the 14th century in the preceding illustration. (The sack of Alost. Bibliothèque Nationale, Paris)

EARNINGS

The standard military rates of pay stayed remarkably consistent over the two centuries and, in fact, the only major change was to the pay of the archers. Both the levied and retained archers were paid at the same rates which in the 14th century were, generally, for a mounted archer 6d a day in England and France, 4d a day in Scotland; for a foot archer 3d a day in England and France, 2d a day in Scotland.[4] There were variations: sometimes ordinary foot archers in England and Wales only got 2d a day whereas selected ones, usually those from Flint and Cheshire who often formed part of the King's personal guard, received 6d a day in all theatres of war. The change came at the beginning of the 15th century when the rates were standardised to 6d a day for both mounted and foot archers both home and abroad except for garrison archers in England, who got 4d a day. It is virtually impossible to translate these rates into modern values, though by way of comparison it can be noted that the pay for a skilled, much-needed ploughman during the manpower shortage immediately after the 'Black Death' was set (though almost always exceeded) by the Statute of Labourers in 1351 at 10 shillings a year.

Burgundian archers in the defensive formation common throughout the period, i.e. backed by billmen and fronted by obstacles - which in this 15th-century example are stakes. (Master Wa, active 1465-85. Private collection. Château de Grandson)

Payment

Indentured soldiers were paid quarterly in advance, though the 'quarter' appears to relate more to the stipulated length of service and not a quarter-year and there is some evidence that payments arranged on a six–week cycle were quite common. Contracts often specified that if payment fell into arrears, some contracts specifing as little as a week, the agreement was annulled and the contracting party was free to depart without blame. Inevitably, in the real world, soldiers sometimes went unpaid for long periods, particularly in Normandy in the 1440s.

It was common practice for retainers to be paid from their doorstep. For example, for a contract between Edward III and Sir Robert Knolles in 1370 the sheriffs were to proclaim that all who would freely set out with Knolles would be '… contented of their wages from the time they should leave their homes… '. Therefore, although the army commander sometimes received the first quarter payment at the signing of the contract with the King or King's Lieutenant, he usually paid the men before receiving any money himself and this is clearly illustrated in an indenture of 1424 between the King and the Earl of Salisbury which stipulates that if a soldier had been killed or died in service, provided the Earl supplied a certificate to that effect, the soldier's wages would not be withheld.

Generally, the first payment made by the King's commissioners to the army commander was at the first muster that was made in their presence, obviously to ensure that the number and quality of the men matched up to what was promised. Likewise, for all subsequent quarterly payments the troops were mustered and inspected and this meant that the commissioners had to travel to wherever the men were serving. Furthermore, if a soldier was absent because of

---

4 This is the pre-decimal English currency of 12d (pence) to 1s (shilling) and 20s to £1.

illness, the commissioners had to travel to wherever that soldier was and, having verified his condition, payment was made. If the commissioners refused to make the journey, payment could still be made in exchange for a certificate . In all contracts, any other absence from military duty, even if authorised, meant a reduction in payment. Of course, the daily wage was not the only income for the indentured archer. If he was a household man or retainer he was also paid an annuity, an amount that varied according to the wealth and generosity of his employer. In the well-known example of Daniel, a household archer of Sir John Howard, he received in 1467 an annuity of £10 (a considerable sum) as well as gifts of clothing and a '... house for his wife to dwell in at Stoke...'. Even hired retainers were paid bonuses, as illustrated by a letter Roger L'Estrange wrote to Sir John Paston in 1492 requesting help in obtaining two or three archers who would be paid '... the Kings wages and some what else, so that I trust they shall be pleased... '. Commanders were well aware of the dangers of the less scrupulous soldier enlisting in one retinue, receiving payment and then deserting, perhaps to appear later in another retinue for a different campaign and, as far as possible, steps were taken to prevent this.

Levied archers raised by Commission of Array were expected to serve unpaid within their own county. During the 14th century, when eligible for service overseas, they were paid by the authorities from the time they crossed over the county boundary until they reached the main army and the first muster when they went onto the King's payroll. In practice the county usually paid them in advance to cover the whole journey and, depending on the generosity of the authorities, could also grant extra travelling money. In the 15th century, though no longer obliged to raise men for foreign service, the county had to pay their soldiers wages for the duration of any domestic campaign outside of the boundary (it should be noted that this only applied to the number of men agreed with the King. The King could, if he required, instruct a county or city to find extra men for whom he would pay the wages). This meant that they were raised and disbanded very quickly and therefore the payment intervals were different. In the case of the archers from the City of York sent for service in Scotland in 1482, they were enlisted for one month and were to receive 14 days money at the muster on the day of departure with the two appointed captains keeping the remaining money to pay out at their discretion. Come the muster, the archers refused to ride unless they received the whole month's money. The authorities had no option but to acquiesce. Three weeks later the city had to send extra wages to their archers in Scotland who were reported to be '... deselet of money... '. A 1424 indenture between the King and the Earl of Salisbury identifies another ploy by the unscrupulous soldier, that of a resident in France, and therefore someone liable for unpaid service in his area under the Array system,who chose, when a campaign was imminent, to enlist in a retinue. If this was discovered to have happened, the guilty party was to repay all wages he had received and if he no longer had the money, to be put in gaol until due restitution was made.

BELOW & OPPOSITE **Baies (underpants) and shirts are pictured as being of the same style no matter the class of the wearer (as is true today) and always white. Invariably of linen, though variations in quality would reflect the status of the wearer. It is not known to what extent braies were worn but pictorial evidence indicates they were a common item. (Drawing © G.A. Embleton)**

PLUNDER

Both retained and levied archers also profited by ransom and plunder. The rules regarding the spoils were plainly laid out. Certain people, if captured, were to be handed over to the King or his lieutenant immediately. This applied to the enemy king, prince or captain of the blood royal, or their lieutenants, marshals and constables. The captor was then granted a suitable reward. All other persons and possessions could be ransomed and sold by their captor but the rewards were to be divided as follows: of the sum raised, one third to go to the captor's immediate captain; of that third, one third to the overall commander; and of that third, one third to the King. This system extended into the frontier garrisons even during relatively peaceful times. In his quarterly report on the garrison of Tomberlaine between December 1443 and March 1444, the clerk to the controller of the garrison recorded the arrivals, departures and periods of absence of the men-at-arms and archers and listed the ransom of a prisoner and the sale of a captured horse and sword. The prize money totalled £28 17s 6d and of this money £9 12s 6d was allocated to the 'lances' (as captains); of that money £3 4s 2d was allocated to the garrison commander and of that money £1 1s 5d was allocated to the King.

Of course, not all plunder was reported by the soldiers. Froissart records how in 1346 the men on campaign in Normandy dutifully reported to their officers the amount of corn, number of houses, horses, cattle and other beasts but '... made no count to the King nor to none of his officers of the gold and silver they did get, they kept that to themselves... '. Froissart's chronicle is full of reports of returning armies laden with 'gold, silver and prisoners' and a chronicler wrote that in 1348 in England '... there were few women who did not possess something from Caen, Calais or other overseas towns, such as clothing, furs, cushions. Table cloths and linen were seen in everybodys' houses... '. One of the lesser known logistic achievements of the Hundred Years War is how all this captured wealth was successfully transported back to England.

VICTUALLING

The English were renowned for their great appetites. So much so that in circa 1500 a Venetian diplomat could report '... But I have it on the best information that when war is raging most furiously they will seek for good eating and all their other comforts without thinking of what harm might befall them... '. The basic foodstuffs were mutton, beef, pork (often salted), oats, peas, beans, cheese, fish (usually saltfish or herrings) and bread. Of equal importance to an Englishman was his quota of ale or beer and a common allowance was one gallon per man per day. It is clear that the individual soldier was expected to pay for his own food and the allowance for that was included in his daily pay. If, alternatively, he was permitted to take it for himself or was free-issued with rations, then his wage was correspondingly lower. Hence the lesser wage paid to soldiers in Scotland in the 14th century and to garrison troops in England in the 15th. The soldier obtained his food by buying it in a market place set up for that purpose (under the jurisdiction of an official often, perhaps always, known as the 'Clerk of the Market') in the camp. The market was supplied with foodstuffs through two methods, themselves a reflection of the levy/indenture system. The first method was 'purveyance', the royal prerogative whereby the King purchased food and livestock at a price guaranteed to be fair but stipulated by his officials. Either merchants

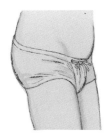

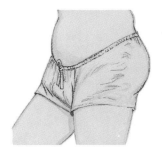

and traders were instructed to deliver the foodstuffs to the camp, or officials known as 'purveyors' were appointed to buy, assemble and deliver the merchandise. Usually a combination of both was used. Everything was delivered to the 'Receiver of Victuals' and accounted for in receipts. The second method was for merchants to sign commercial indentures with the King or his Lieutenant undertaking to supply victuals for sale in 'open market'. These indentures could be quite rigid and stipulated what food was to be supplied, where and when. For the 1415 campaign Henry V instructed the sheriffs of Southampton on 27 May to ensure the relevant tradesmen in Southampton, Winchester and the adjoining areas '… shall bake and brew…' under their supervision so that sufficient provision would be available when the army mustered for embarkation. On 24th. June the sheriffs were further instructed to arrange for the assembly of '…oxen, calves and cows to the number of one hundred animals… ' that could be sold to the 'lords and others' of the army at a price agreed between the owners and the purchasers. And on the 24th. July it was proclaimed that each lord, knight, esquire, valet and all others should provide himself with victuals and necessities for the 'voyage' for a quarter of a year.

The market system was not restricted to camps in England. Either because the local countryside had already been stripped bare or because the King or commander did not want to antagonise the local population, English provisions also reached camps and siege lines in France and Scotland. The victualling for the English siege of Calais in 1347 was conducted entirely from England and in 1418 Henry V wrote to the Mayor and Aldermen of London asking that small boats be loaded with food and drink, cross to Harfleur and then sail up the Seine to his siege of Rouen. Victuallers travelling abroad were given armed escorts in hostile areas and archers were often assigned to such duties. In case temptation proved too strong for anybody, there was a mandatory death sentence for the robbing of any victualler travelling to and from the army. There is, as yet, little information on the criteria used for issuing the food collected and brought in by troops out foraging, though we do know the foragers were usually allowed to keep a portion of their 'harvest'. It is likely that the distribution of the balance was organised by the 'Receiver of Victuals' and probably simply allocated to the camps' market place. Inevitably there were occasions when food was in short supply. Jean Le Bels' account of the 1359 French expedition records how the English were '… in great straits for bread, wine, meat… ' because the countryside had been laid bare and it '… rained constantly day and night… '. Because of the haste with which the Yorkist army of the Tewkesbury campaign in 1471 had been assembled and despatched, there was no time for organised victualling. The only food and drink the men received was that given out from the limited supplies Edward IV had brought with him. The lack of water especially caused problems during the forced marches of that hot, summer campaign. Unsurprisingly, food deteriorated. This was usually because of the length of time it had been in store or through salt water contamination during transportation. In these cases the food was sold cheaply or, if too bad, destroyed. There must have been occasions when unscrupulous

BELOW & OPPOSITE **These drawings illustrate the basic changes in doublet and hose from the 14th to the 16th century, i.e.the lifting of the hem line and from 'single-leg' to 'joined' hose. 'A' and 'B' show the different seam lines of joined hose, though 'A' is less common. Also detailed are the two patterns for fitting hose around the foot. Doublet sleeves were simple up to the mid-15th century, after that 'puffed' (padded) shoulders bacame a common feature on soldiers. Collars, if fitted, were always high with a 'U' or 'V' shaped seam. Hose was fastened to**

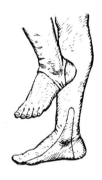

A

B

merchants and officials sold or supplied unfit food to the men, but, by and large, the victualling system seems to have been controlled well and, although there are records of malpractice by some officials, e.g. the purveyors, there is no great evidence of widespread corruption.

Unfortunately, there are no descriptions of the day-to-day mechanics of cooking and eating and whether each soldier bought and cooked his own or someone in the contingent was designated to do it. The household relationship may have played some part, and certainly garrison soldiers would have had food cooked and issued on that system, but just how many men, if any, of a retinue benefited from the portable ovens most lords had transported with them is not known. Cooking arrangements were probably as fluid as they have always been.

UNIT FORMATION

A large army marched and fought in three 'Battles' or 'Wards', the Vanward, the Main (or Middle) ward and the Rearward, each with its own commander and second-in-command. The overall commander was usually also the commander of the Mainward. It was the task of the Constable and Marshals to arrange the battles and allocate the retinues and, if applicable, the levies. With smaller forces the senior officers performed the task. As to deployment, the Commissions of Array record how the men of the levy were organised into 'twenties', 'hundreds' and, if the numbers warranted it, 'thousands'. The twenty consisted of nineteen men under a 'vintenar', five of these made a hundred under a 'centenar' and ten of these made the thousand under a 'millenar'. By the second half of the 15th century the centenar was more often known as a captain, often with one or more 'petty-captains' to assist him. In fact, captain became a very common term and could be applied to any commander, noble or commoner, of a body of any number of men. Companies of specialist indentured troops, i.e. miners, were also organised into twenties and hundreds as were any extra companies of archers contracted outside of the retinues. However, the system with the indentured retinues may have been very different and much research has still to be done into the organisation of the English armies of the period. One question is whether the small retinues were just an instrument for recruiting and mobilising men, or whether they were also considered a unit formation in their own right. That a 'relationship' continued is indicated by the clerk's division of ransom in the Tomberlaine garrison (see 'Earnings') where he lists entries such as '…John Flourison archer to Richard Harper, a mounted lance… '. It may be that small 'sub-contracting' units were assembled under the charge of their employer who placed himself under the command of his employer. But, while we know that the men-at-arms and archers were separated from their units and grouped together, as at Agincourt when all the archers were placed under the overall command of Sir Thomas Erphingham, at present we can only speculate as to how these men were then officered.

It is usual for historians to discuss the ratio of archers to men-at-arms and how it grew from about 1:1 in the middle of the 14th century to 3:1, then 5:1 and over. The oft-quoted Teller's Roll for the 1475 French expedition indicates a ratio averaging 8:1 and this has been offered as evidence of a 'drying-up' of men-at-arms and consequent decline in the overall quality of the English army from the middle of the 15th century.[5] But these figures are an over-simplification and

---

5 See, for example, J. R. Lander, *'The Hundred Years War and Edward IV's 1474 Campaign in France'*.

should not be taken at their face value. The Teller's Roll, for instance, makes no mention of Billmen and yet they would have been present. Records from the 1330s, when Edward III was establishing the organisation of his armies, show that there was often one mounted and one foot archer to one man-at-arms. From the 1360s onward the relative number of archers increases but there are rarely more than two mounted archers to one man-at-arms and on chevauchees it was usual for only mounted archers to be used. For the 1415 campaign the indentures record the vast majority of retinues as two or three mounted or foot archers to each man-at-arms and subsequent indentures indicate that throughout the 15th century the army in France worked to a ratio of one, two or three mounted archers to each man-at-arms (the latter often accompanied by an attendant). But for major campaigns these retinues were supplemented by large numbers of foot archers. For example, in 1415 Henry V employed companies of archers through direct contracts and in the face of the French threat to Guienne in January 1453 John Talbot, Viscount Lisle, indented for 80 men-at-arms and 800 foot archers and, in July, John Baker indented for 25 men-at-arms and 250 archers. The evidence suggests that any unit was organised for the task in hand with mounted archers featuring predominantly where speed was important (as on *chevauchees)* and in the "permanent" retinues of occupied France. It would therefore not be safe to take, say, Lisle's and Baker's obviously purpose-planned ratio of 10:1 as typical for the armies.

Further, the danger of simply using accounting rolls for ascertaining the composition of any army is highlighted by an indenture of 1428 between Thomas, Earl of Salisbury and the King. This starts by contracting for 600 men-at-arms and 1,800 mounted archers but goes on to state that the Earl has the option of replacing four men-at-arms by four master artillerymen and ten archers by ten miners (to be paid 20d and 9d respectively. The Earl would still only receive the 12d and 6d allowance for them and the King would make up the difference directly) or replacing 200 men-at-arms with 600 archers (or any such proportion) or having 70 or 80 .'…persons, craftsmen such as carpenters, masons, bowyers, fletchers and such other workmen required for the war who, although they possibly may not as yet be good bowmen, shall nevertheless be passed at musters, and shall have their wages, as archers… '. Therefore, while any Teller's Roll or similar would simply record payment for 1,800 archers and 600 men-at-arms (3:1) we know that the force might have in fact been composed of 2,400 archers and 400 men-at-arms (6:1) or 596 men-at-arms, four master artillerymen, 1,710 archers, and ten miners – or any combination of the above.

Tactical formation

Because they were usually outnumbered, the English fought their major battles against the French in defensive formations, Castillon being a notable exception, and though these require a lesser degree of control than a battle of movement, nevertheless the chroniclers record a high level of discipline. At Crecy Froissart describes how the English, allocated into three 'Battles', were lying on the ground, resting, when .'…as soon as they saw the Frenchmen approach, they rose upon their feet fair and easily without any haste and arranged their

Hats were worn by all classes of society and considered a necessary part of a man's clothing. When he was not wearing a helmet, an archer would invariably have put on a hat. There was such a variety of styles that it is almost impossible to outline every possibility, but shown here are some of the most common types. (Drawing © G.A. Embleton)

battles'. Even in the heat of combat 'the Englishmen would not issue out of their battle for taking of any prisoner'.

In defensive positions archers always made use of any natural obstacles – ditches, hedges, vineyards, sunken roads etc. – or constructed their own – dykes, palisades, and their famous stakes. At Agincourt the stakes were rough-cut on the march and carried by the archers themselves as there was rumour of a surprise attack by French horse, but later references show they became an accepted part of transported military stores and much more sophisticated with iron heads, sockets, rings and staples. During sieges archers were often instructed to prepare and carry bundles of faggots for filling up the enemy's defensive ditches and these were sometimes piled together and used as temporary defensive screens.

It is clear that the archers did most of the manual work themselves. The anonymous priest, eyewitness of Harfleur and Agincourt, records how the Duke of Clarence oversaw the construction of one approach trench at Harfleur where .'…he caused this trench moreover to be constructed by his lancemen and bowmen, having appointed masters of the works, and assigned certain feet of ground to each lance and to each bow, until the whole work was entirely accomplished'.

The archers always worked in conjunction with the dismounted men-at-arms and billmen, though there is disagreement among modern historians over exactly how this was done. Froissart tells us that their formation was called a 'hearse' which has been taken to be an allusion to the medieval agricultural harrow (often triangular) and the assumption has been that the archers were placed on the wings of the other footmen to give each Battle a flat-bottomed 'V' shape, the archers then shooting into the flanks of the attacking force. However, the evidence actually suggests that, in defence, the archers were placed in front of the footmen. For instance, Froissart on Crecy: .'…certain Frenchmen and Almains perforce opened the archers of the princes battle and came and fought with the men of arms hand to hand… ' and on Poitiers: .'…At the end of this hedge among vines and thorn bushes, where no man can go nor ride, are their men of arms all afoot, and they have set in front of them their archers in manner of a herse… '; the Sire de Remy, eyewitness at Agincourt: .'…the King of England appointed an old knight, called Sir Thomas Erpingham, to draw up unobserved the archers and to place them in front… '; and the anonymous chronicler of Stoke in 1487: '… wher the King sett his folks in array of batell, that is to say, a bow and a bill at his bak… '. Conversely, for an advance there is at least one reference (**see 'Behaviour'**) to the men-at-arms proceeding in front of the archers.

DEFENSIVE WEAR AND WEAPONS

For the majority of archers the predominant defensive wear was a padded garment known in the 14th century as a *gambeson* (or *aketon*) and in the 15th as the *jack*. These were quilted coats constructed either of layers of fabric or an outer and inner layer stuffed with other material. The best fabric to use was *fustian,* an extremely strong cloth made of a linen warp with a cotton weft, woven in a twill weave and cut to give a thick, low pile.

The *gambeson* was knee length with substantial sleeves narrowing towards the wrist and stitching that ran vertically. By the middle of the next century the *jack* had shortened to thigh length and horizontal stitching was often added to the vertical to give a squared pattern, or diagonal used to give a diamond pattern. Most *jacks* were sleeved, though sometimes these were detachable. Because of the thickness of *jacks*, doublets were not worn and so, to hold the hose up, a

ABOVE **There does not appear to have been any military regulations covering hairstyles. Generally hair was medium length, though as in all periods, some soldiers preferred the convenience of short 'crew-cuts'. English soldiers are virtually always portrayed as clean shaven, but how often they shaved and whether there was any military stipulation is simply not known.**
(Drawing © G.A. Embleton)

Drawn here are some of the many kinds of shoes and boots typical of those worn by soldiers. As with hats, there are far too many variations to list and fashions remained in use for many years. Generally the rougher the occupation the stouter the shoe and the less pointed the toe. (Drawing ©. G.A. Embleton)

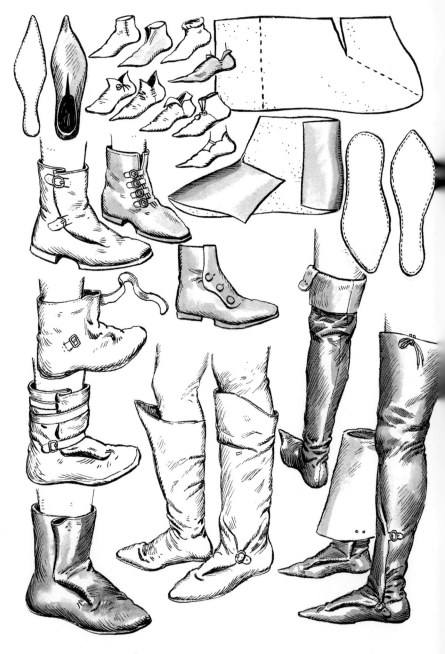

waistcoat-type garment known as a *pourpoint* (for obvious reasons) was used – and perhaps had been worn under the *gambeson* as well, but there is no evidence for this.

These garments were worn either on their own or over or under the second most common defence: 'mail'.[6] Mail shirts could be either hip, thigh or knee length with either half, three-quarter or full-length sleeves. Some 15th century *jacks* incorporated an internal layer of mail. Sir John Fastolfs' will of 1459 lists some *jacks* 'stuffed' with mail and some with horn plates. The wearing of padding with mail was not done purely for comfort, for a blow on mail unbacked by substantial fabric will still break the bone or drive the rings into the flesh. Modern tests have also verified contemporary accounts of the relative effectiveness of a

---

6 Note that it is not 'chainmail'. This is a modernism. 'Mail' derives from the old French *maille* = a net.

mail/*jack* combination against arrows. There is no evidence at all for mail leggings being worn by archers in this period but there are a few illustrations of mail 'shorts'.

In the 15th century, with the increased use of plate armour, a thinner version of the jack known as the *arming doublet* was worn by men-at-arms under their armour and which had points to which the armour was attached. Sometimes arming doublets had pieces of mail sewn on to cover areas left exposed by armour and mail-covered sleeves, this removed the need to wear a full mail shirt. It is likely that some household archers wore these doublets (as the Scottish archer guard certainly did). These garments also functioned as a true doublet in that they held the hose up (and there are records of *arming hose*) and the best quality ones were sometimes lined with a soft material, such as silk, so as to be worn without the need for a shirt.

During the 14th century many knights had worn the *coat-of-plates*, basically a poncho-like garment of some strong material with strap fastenings from front to back and large internal plates riveted to the fabric. There is no evidence that archers wore these but by the second half of the 15th century they did wear it's successor, the *brigandine*. This was a jacket, nearly always sleeveless, with internal flexible layers of overlapping small metal plates fixed to the material by a series of rivets called 'nails', invariably set in a triangle of three with the heads left exposed. Often referred to as a *pair of brigandines*, they fastened most commonly by buckles and straps down the front, though occasionally along the shoulders and down the sides and sometimes with laces. There were wide variations in quality, the best being good enough to be worn by royalty and the nobility. The Beauchamp Pageant shows what appears to be *brigandines* of fewer, larger plates held by fewer, larger rivets. Contemporary paintings show some archers wearing a surprising amount of plate armour. While it is perfectly possible to shoot in a back & breast and a helmet, it is difficult to imagine shooting whilst wearing full arm defences and a *bevor* (a chin/throat protector). However, this is to look at it with a modern eye and without the benefit of the constant usage and archery upbringing our forefathers had. Many household men and retainers would have had some form of plate arm and leg defences even if only of 'munition standard'.

For helmets, 14th and early 15th century archers wore either the all-metal open-faced *bascinet*, occasionally with a mail *aventail* (a chin/neck guard, sus-

Though Flemish and dating from a little after our period, nevertheless this picture represents a scene that must have been very common in any village in England. The archers shooting between these butts (which seem to be of padded timber) appear to have a remarkably carefree attitude about the safety of the livestock and spectators! (*The Fair at Hoboken* by Bruegel. Boymans van Beuningen Museum, Rotterdam)

pended from the helmet rim) or a conical cap either of one-piece metal or of overlapping, laminated plates of metal, horn or whalebone. From the 1450s the *sallet* predominated, in a variety of forms, usually open-faced but sometimes with a visor. Fastolf's will also listed caps stuffed with mail or horn.

For arms the archer had a dagger, some type of sword and a small, round shield known as the *buckler*. The English were renowned for their sword-and-buckler fencing up to the 17th century. Later writers describe the archers as always equipped with a *maul*, an iron or lead-headed long-handled mallet, but though contemporary writers describe this weapon it is one amongst many – and used by all classes. It is clear from battle accounts that, when hand-to-hand fighting got desperate, archers grabbed anything that came to hand. Charles the Bold of Burgundy did instruct his archers to carry *mauls* but it seems they were to be used to hammer in the stakes they were also supposed to transport – in direct imitation of the English.

Livery

Through both centuries the archer wore the badge and colours of his employer – whether lord, gentry or city. Sometimes the badge alone was used but it was

Illustrated here are various types of 15th-century jacks. The sleeves were often less thickly padded than the body and to facilitate movement there were sometimes slits in the crease of the elbow and a gap under the armpit. Varying arrangements of chains were occasionally laced and/or stitched down the outside of the arms as an extra protection against sword cuts. (Drawing © G.A. Embleton)

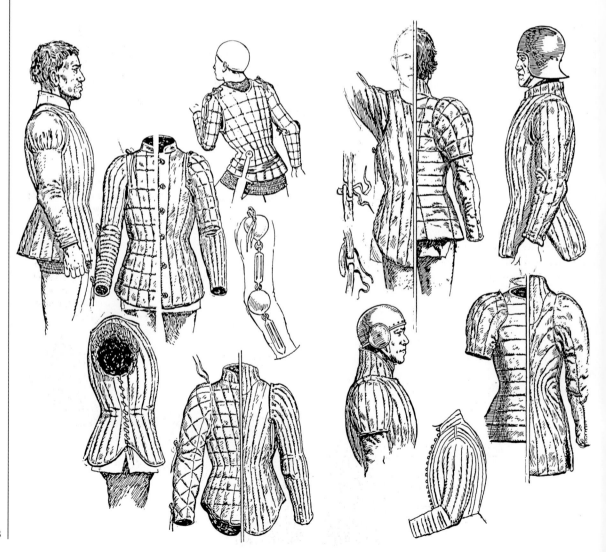

common for livery[7] coats or jackets to be worn and these can be seen as the ancestor of uniform. Contemporary accounts are contradictory in their description of the two and a variety of styles are illustrated, so, for convenience, the author takes 'coat' to mean a substantial garment, fully·sleeved, with or without a collar, while 'jacket' as being a simpler article, always collarless, occasionally half-sleeved but usually sleeveless. Both garments either hip or thigh length and made of wool (though perhaps of linen for hot climates). To judge by their stiff appearance they were lined or made with a very thick broadcloth and, in the absence of any evidence of laces, were fastened by buttons (covered in material of the same colour) or, probably more common, hooks and eyes.

Badges were sewn or embroidered onto the coat and jacket. For jackets they were usually large enough to cover most of the front and repeated on the back. For coats, and no doubt some jackets as well, they were smaller and worn on the left breast, with or without a larger one on the back. The Beauchamp Pageant shows the Earl's attendants either in jackets with a Ragged Staff badge front and back, or in short coats with the badge only on the back. A few illustrations show other servants, messengers and musicians, wearing what appear to be small metal badges on the left breast. A panel of the famous 14th century Wilton Diptych depicts the angels wearing Richard II's badge of the White Hart and these seem to be metal, enamelled and gilded. From at least the 1440s it was also a fashion for 'domestic' livery coats to have the badge embroidered onto the outside of the left sleeve, as the Great Chronicle of London records in the entry for 1443: '...for in those dayes & long afftyr every lordys lyverey & servauntys were known by the conysaunce brawderid upon thyr sleve'.

Edward I seems to have been the first king to issue the Cross of St. George to his soldiers as the identifying badge of the English. For much of the period under discussion this was of varying sizes and sewn directly onto top garments or glued or painted onto breastplates. Campaign regulations made this compulsory and decreed the death penalty for any of the enemy who were caught wearing it. One of Henry V's regulations for the 1415 campaign stated that if an Englishman mistakenly killed another Englishman because the latter had neglected to wear the cross he would have no charge to answer – a rule which probably

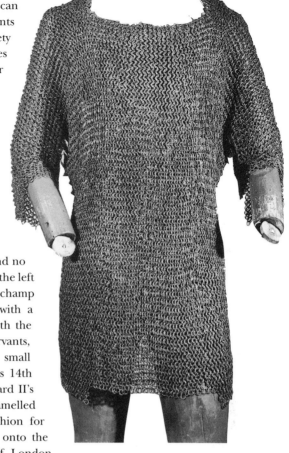

ABOVE **Mail shirt. German c. 1430. (A4735/10 III 1320. Board of Trustees of the Royal Armouries)**

BELOW **Pair of mail sleeves for attaching to an arming doublet. Late 15th/early 16th century. (A11/221 III 1427/1428. Board of Trustees of the Royal Armouries)**

---

7 The free issue of any item – food, clothing, equipment, etc. – to a servant. From the old French *livree* – an allowance.

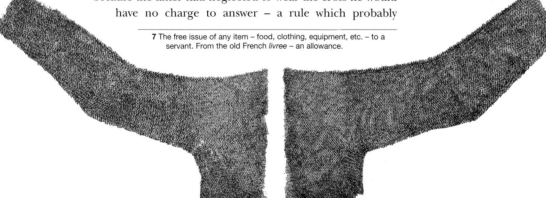

followed earlier precedents. From about the middle of the 15th century English archers are increasingly pictured wearing white jackets with a large St. George's Cross both front and Back. For the Scottish campaign of 1481 Edward IV decreed that *all* soldiers were to '... have uppon hym a white Jaket with a crosse of Seynt George swed theruppon... ' but permitted any individual who so wished to also wear the badge of the captain with whom he had enlisted. As the Teller's Roll for the 1475 expedition lists the badges of the individual captains, it is almost certain that the same arrangement was laid down for that campaign as well. These badges would have been worn on the left breast.

We can only guess at how well informed the average soldier was on the identification of individual badges, something made more difficult by many lords adopting more than one through marriage into and inheritance of different estates. For example, Richard Duke of York, father of Edward IV, had badges of the white rose, the falcon and fetterlock, a white lion, a black bull and a black dragon. The soldiers of an assembled force of his retainers may possibly have displayed all the different badges of their respective estates. It was because of this that a single, common emblem was sometimes adopted. The White Rose of York became the symbol of the Yorkist faction and used by all its leaders and at the second battle of St. Albans in 1461, the Lancastrians besides wearing their own lords' livery, '... every man and lorde bore the Pryncys leverey that was a bende of crymesyn and blacke with eterygeys (ostrich) fetherys... ' – the Prince being Henry VI's son. It was also the case that, because of the fame of the individual or the longevity of use, some badges became very well known, like the Bear and/or Ragged Staff of Warwick the Kingmaker and the Crescent Moon of the Percies.

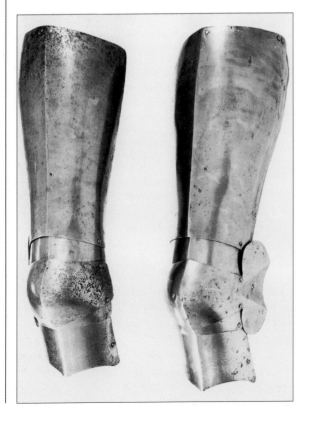

Pair of cuisses and poleynes for the legs. Italian (?) c. 1420. (A4855/188 III 1285/1286. Board of Trustees of the Royal Armouries)

Issue

Arms, armour, equipment and livery were supplied to the household man and the retainer by his employer. This supplemented, or replaced, whatever he might personally possess. The household account books of Sir John Howard have, for the period of the proposed Scottish campaign in 1480, numerous entries for the issuing to his, named, retained archers the following set of equipment: '... a peir brigandines, a peir splentes, a salate, a standart, his jaket, a gusset...'.[8] It would appear from the above account books that Howard kept the equipment and livery in stock and issued them when required, which we must assume was a standard practise for senior commanders. When rebellion broke out in England in 1469, Edward IV, in Norwich, sent to the office of the 'Wardrobe' in London for 1,000 jackets of blue and murray with white roses. Household men, of course, would have been in permanent possession of their equipment and livery.

The levy were supplied with arms, armour, equipment and livery at their county's, or city's, expense. The equipment provided for archers consisted of bows, one sheaf of arrows per man and 'competent arms' which usually meant swords and

---

8 splints = simple arm defences of plate; a standard = a neck defence of mail; jaket = his livery; gusset = ?unknown. The brigandines issued here were probably of the simpler type described elsewhere

knives. Details of 14th century livery are extremely scarce; the only known example of colour is that of the soldiers of the two adjoining counties of Flint and Cheshire. In their case, whenever the men were levied, each was given a short coat and a hood, both of wool and green on the right side and white on the left. It was the task of the Chamberlain of Chester to buy the cloth, have the coats and hoods made up and delivered to the men. On one occasion when the men of Flint were arrayed at short notice they received their livery in London. There is no record of a badge.

There are far more details of livery for the levy during the 15th century, but reasons for the choice of a particular colour are often obscure. In 1470 a contingent of levied men from Canterbury was posted to the garrison at Calais. They were supplied with jackets of a red cloth (which must have been of good quality as it cost three shillings a yard) and bearing white roses made of 'karsey' (a coarse, ribbed woollen cloth). No doubt the white rose was used because it was the badge of the King, Edward IV, but we can only speculate as to why the colour red – whether because it was the most commonly available cloth, or because it was Canterbury's colour, or because it was Warwick's colour and, though at that time in rebellion against the King, he was still technically Captain of Calais. In 1461 a contingent from Rye which went to join his army also wore red.

WEAPONS

The Bow

The 'longbow' has now become so entrenched in history it is usually overlooked that it did not represent the only design of bow in use in medieval Europe. Retained and levied archers would be carrying their own bows when enlisted but would be re-equipped by the army – contemporary records show the 'wastage' rate to have been enormous. And as the English army changed from one raised by feudal obligation to one of indentured and paid service raised under central government control, it was inevitable that the government, in the shape of the then war department, the office of the 'Ordnance', would become increasingly responsible for supplying all manner of equipment and, just as today, much of that equipment was made to a government standard.

Lower canon for the left arm. Italian c. 1500. (A3/2446 III 1113. Board of Trustees of the Royal Armouries)

The 'long bow' represents the design chosen for military service because, though not technically the most efficient bow of the period, it admirably suited the demands made upon it, i.e. for a relatively cheap, though well–made, robust weapon suitable for mass production and capable of projecting a man-stopping missile over a good distance at a fast 'rate of fire' – exactly the same criteria laid down for every infantry weapon up to the present day. It is unlikely that the archer would have normally called his weapon a 'longbow'. The earliest references to the word are from the 15th century and used in listings of equipment to differentiate them from crossbows. On their own they are simply called 'bowes'. It was not until later in the 16th century that 'longbow' (written as one word or two) becomes common and identified with a particular type. The contemporary title for it was 'livery bow' as the issuing of weapons to the soldiers by the 'Ordnance' office was simply seen as an extension to that system. It is a matter for argument as to whether the military adopted a bow already in common usage in civilian England or vice-versa but this bow became so widespread in English society it was also known in Europe as the 'English bow'.

The War Bow

The war bow was what we call today a 'self-bow', i.e. made from one piece of wood, and for these bows the best timber is yew. This has been known since prehistoric times although, for reasons of availability, other timbers have always been used. Alternatives in the Middle Ages were: ash, elm and wych (wych elm, also then called – confusingly – wych hazel) and from the 15th century brazil, imported from the East. There is also one 15th century reference to 'auburne' (laburnum). But the principal timber for English war bows was yew with wych elm a poor second.

The bowstaves were taken from the trunk of the tree, the primary branches or the sapling. Contemporary accounts value the trunk highest but to meet the huge demand the principal source was the primary branches and the staves can only have come from carefully tended, pollarded trees in purpose-grown and maintained plantations. England imported yew bowstaves from throughout Europe and though native timber was also used it was never highly regarded. The best yew originally came from Spain but following the destruction of the country's stocks by it's king during the Anglo-Spanish wars of the late 14th century, the best obtainable was from Italy and by the middle of the 15th century Venice had become the main export centre for bowstaves which were usually bought, stored and shipped by resident English merchants.

A later description records bowstaves as being: '…three fingers thick and squared and seven feet long, to be well got up, polished and without knots'.[9] Wherever the origin of the staves, they were always examined by English officials, sorted for quality and marked accordingly. The recovered *Mary Rose* bows show that everybody, from growers through to examiners, did their job well as these bows are made from a quality of yew simply unobtainable today.

Self-bows consist of both the heartwood and a thinner layer of sapwood. The heartwood becomes the 'belly' of the bow and the sapwood the 'back', so called because of the direction of bend, i.e. the same as the human body. The optimum length for a finished bow is between 5' 7" and 6' 2" but the *Mary Rose* bows are some 3" to 4" longer and a statute of 1465 dictates that Englishmen living in Ireland .'…betwixt sixty and sixteen in age shal have an English bow of his own length and one fistmele at the least between the nyckes'.[10] This appears to have been done for safety as Sir John Smythe was later to write '… in times past… there was special care had that all Liveray or warre bows being of the wood of

ABOVE AND RIGHT **Exterior and interior rear view of a 15th-century brigandine. This is the most common type and appears frequently in illustrations. This example fastens down the front and along the shoulders by straps and buckles. (A11/802 & A12/445 III 1663. Board of Trustees of the Royal Armouries)**

---

9 Richard Galloway could fashion a bow from such a stave in just 1 3/4 hours, which gives some idea of the possible production rate. **10** A 'fistmele' equals about 4". This dispels the notion that medieval man was considerably shorter than his descendant. Excavated skeletons have shown that the average height was 5' 6" – and this same average lasted up to the 1940s. It is only the improved social and dietary conditions of the last fifty years that have caused a marked difference. However, many archers, especially household ones, would have been picked for their size. The skeletons recovered from the Mary Rose average 5' 8" and include one archer who was at least 6' tall.

Yewgh were longer that they now use them... that they seldome or never brake'.

The optimum cross-section of the limbs is of a rounded 'D' and the draw-weight (the amount of pulling power needed) anywhere between 80lbs to 120lbs. Modern tests have shown that with this type of bow there is no real advantage in increasing the draw-weight over 120lbs, but that's not to say this was never done. (Note that modern target bows have a draw-weight of around 45lbs and that of modern longbows is between 40 – 60lbs).

Contrary to popular belief, the bow is not always made from a straight stave. New yew bows often have a forward curve, like a shallow 'C' (the modern term is 'reflexed'), because of the natural tendency of the stave's heartwood grain to expand. While this feature is disguised when the bow is strung, the forces that cause it work to the benefit of the bow's performance. Inevitably, this feature gradually disappears the more often the bow is drawn back until, on well- used bows, the curve is reversed and the bow is said to have 'followed the string'. Bowyers sometimes used a heat treatment to put an increased curve into the ends of the bow limbs, which Ascham called 'whipping' (the modern term is 'recurved'). This increases the allowable draw-length (the distance the bow can be pulled back) and noticeably improves the bow's performance. Many of the recovered *Mary Rose* bows have reflexed, recurved and 'string-follow' characteristics.

It is clear from medieval illustrations and from the *Mary Rose* survivors that war bows were tipped with horn nocks on which the string loops fitted. This was done primarily to protect the limb tips though it also assists the stringing of the bow by allowing for a larger string loop, enabling it to slide up and down the bow limb.

It is also clear that no handle bindings were used. The earliest reference the author has seen showing *any* European bow with such a binding is Flemish and dates from circa 1565. Ascham recommended the waxing of the centre of the bow to stop the heat and moisture from the hand spoiling the wood. The *Mary Rose* bows have stamped marks at the bow centre which was no doubt a common

Two Milanese sallets c. 1450 and 1500. The one on the left is very similar in shape to those worn by the archers in the Beauchamp Pagent. (A214/4 IV 741 & 424. Board of Trustees of the Royal Armouries)

BELOW **A view of the lining of a sallet. Based on a drawing in an article 'A late medieval helmet (sallet)' by Stephen V. Grancsay of the Metropolitan Museum of Art, New York. (Drawing c G.A. Embleton)**

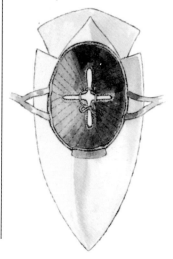

practice and which, as well as being the bowyers' mark, also possibly indicated where the arrow should be shot from. Consistency here was important for both accuracy and safety. Unlike modern bows there was no distinct top and bottom limbs and these bows were designed to be shot either way up.

Finished bows were supplied as 'painted' or 'white', i.e. with or without a wax or polished finish. During times of military preparation the government not only bought up all the available stocks of bows and bowstaves, they also conscripted the bowyers. In an example from 1359, one William de Rothwell was ordered to '… take in London and elsewhere as many armourers, fletchers, smiths and other artificers and workmen as are required for the making of armour, bows, bowstrings, arrows, arrowheads… and put them to work at the King's wages'.

Along with armourers and other artificers, bowyers accompanied the army on the march, though surprisingly for such a skilled job, they were only paid at the same rate as the archers.

Arrows

Many people have heard of the famous 'clothyard' arrow. Unfortunately, this term is a literary invention. The description is a misquotation from a ballad of circa 1465 spread into literature by 17th century balladeers and poets. There is no historical justification for it and much erroneous research has been done into the length of the clothyard in order to establish a length for the war arrow.

War arrows were known as 'Livery', 'Sheaf' or 'Standard'. Livery because they were issued; Sheaf from the Anglo-Saxon word for a bundle, or perhaps because 24 or 30 arrows tied together look like a sheaf of grain; Standard either because they were made to the length of the legal standard yard or, more probably, because the whole design was subject to a government specification. They were of a large diameter so they could carry a large head to do maximum damage. Because of this it is preferable they be of a light timber to reduce weight and they are described in contemporary documents and by Ascham as made of 'aspe', i.e. aspen (*Populus tremula*) which is indeed ideal for mass-produced arrows. The trees, grown in wet conditions, are easily propagated from cuttings, extremely fast growing and produce a timber both light and strong.

However, medieval herbals are contradictory in their definition of 'aspe' and it may have been used as a generic word for all the native poplars. Ash arrows also appear on medieval inventories and Ascham actually recommends ash for war arrows on the supposition that, being heavier, they would give a 'greater stripe', ie. hit harder. But as he wrote *some* ash it must have been as true then as it is now that suitable ash is difficult to obtain and producing arrowshafts involves a lot of wastage. And on large-diameter arrows the weight of ash does make a considerable difference to performance. Perhaps heavy shafts were for use at short ranges. Other timbers were used, Ascham lists fifteen, and it has been reported that arrowshafts of aspen, alder, elder, birch, willow and the heavier ash and hornbeam have been recovered from the *Mary Rose*. These are all on Ascham's list though it is surprising he does not mention that most popular of native trees of 19th and 20th century archery, the Scots Pine (*Pinus sylvestris*).

All the available information on the *Mary Rose* arrows is included in the caption to the accompanying drawing and this can be taken as a description of the typical war arrow of this entire period.

Spare 'ammunition' for the archers was carried in the wagons either contained in chests, which were sometimes covered in leather, or in that universal container of the Middle Ages, the barrel – often fitted with locks.

A few contemporary illustrations exist showing boxes of arrows without heads next to barrels of heads. It is possible that heads were only 'jammed' on, or perhaps just held on with wax, the advantage of this being the ease with which an arrow could then be recovered from wherever it was embedded, fitted with a new head and used again.

Sir John Smythe, writing in 1590, stated that in every sheaf of 24 arrows, 8 should be lighter 'flight' arrows to 'gall' the enemy at longer distances, but there is no evidence that this was ever actually practised in this period.

Strings

Strings were made of hemp (fibres from plants of the genus *canabis*.) Sir John Smythe wrote '... and the strings being made of verie good hemp, with a kind of water glewe to resist wet and moysture, and the same strings being by the Archers themselves with fine threed well whipt did also verie seldom breake. But if anie such strings in time of service did happen to breake, the soldiers archers had alwaies in readiness a couple of strings more readie whipt and fitted to their bows [i.e. made to measure] to clappe on in an instant. And this I have heard of divers Yeoman that have served as soldiers Archers in the field'.

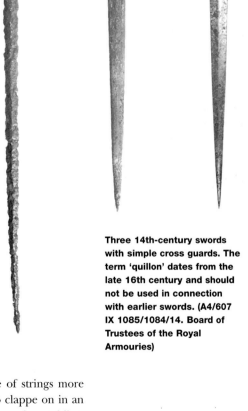

Three 14th-century swords with simple cross guards. The term 'quillon' dates from the late 16th century and should not be used in connection with earlier swords. (A4/607 IX 1085/1084/14. Board of Trustees of the Royal Armouries)

'Well whipt' in the above context is to whip, or wind, some thread around the centre section of the string to protect it from wear caused by the arrow nock and the archer's fingers.

Like all strings and ropes, bowstrings are made from individual strands, though in this case twisted, and not plaited, together. The string loops that fitted on the bow nocks were strengthened by doubling the number of strands in that area. Bowstrings are either made 'double-looped', i.e. one loop for each bow nock, or 'single-looped', though here the 'loose end' is similarly strengthened by doublestranding. In this latter case the archer makes his own loop using a simple timber-hitch known as the 'bowyers knot'. The advantage of the single loop is that, while double-looped strings can only be made for bows when the exact length of limbs is known, on a single-loop string the archer can adjust the position of the lower loop to allow for any bow length. Therefore it is likely that all mass-produced strings for war bows would have been single-looped. During the course of their making the strings were laid in a glue which helped to hold the strands together and, as Smythe noted, made them more moisture resistant – though care has to be taken that these 'laid-in' strings are not allowed to dry out overmuch as this causes the glue to stiffen and crack. Hempen strings made properly are very strong and, though the number of strands is in relation to the strength of the bow, there is no need for even the more powerful bows to have very thick strings. Unfortunately no strings appear to have survived from the *Mary Rose* but the arrow nocks to which they fitted show they were ⅛th. of an inch in diameter. There are medieval references, including Ascham, to bowstrings of flax and silk – and the latter carried a surprisingly high reputation. To what extent these alternatives were actually used is unclear. Flax, also laid in glue, certainly became common during the 18th century and from then until the Second World War the best of them were made in Belgium. Whatever the efficacy of silk strings, they are unlikely to have been available to most military archers!

Bracers, Shooting Gloves and Quivers

The bracer serves two purposes, one is to protect the forearm from the string and the other is to ensure that any loose sleeve fabric is kept from the path of the string. Ideally the string should not hit the arm at all and some archers achieve this by bending the elbow, though this reduces the draw-length. Ascham recommended increasing the 'bracing height' (the distance between bow and string when the bow is strung but not drawn) to a length whereby the string would not reach the forearm on it's travels but, as the bracing height can noticeably affect the shooting characteristics of a bow, this is not a rule-of-thumb that can always be followed.

Bracers were made of leather and horn, occasionally of ivory (medieval ivory often being walrus tooth). Eleven bracers of leather and one of horn were recovered from the *Mary Rose*. The leather ones were basically rectangular, though slightly longer than wider, many with the corners rounded off, and like the Tudor one exhibited in the British Museum, were all decorated. The British Museum and three of the *Mary Rose* examples are engraved with elaborate coats of arms but the others have simply been punched. The punch marks are randomly placed but always either side of the presumed string path. The marks depict simple heraldic badges which may be purely conventional although, as they are often recognisable as badges of guilds, cities or members of the nobility, they might indicate in whose service the archer was employed or recruited. They all fasten by a single strap and buckle (though some may just have been tied),

Sword of the mid-14th to early 16th century. Contrary to popular belief, the development of extra hand guards did not originate in the 16th century. The earliest features, datable to the mid-14th century, are a ring below the cross or a simple 'knuckle-bow'. (A12/976 IX 2639. Board of Trustees of the Royal Armouries)

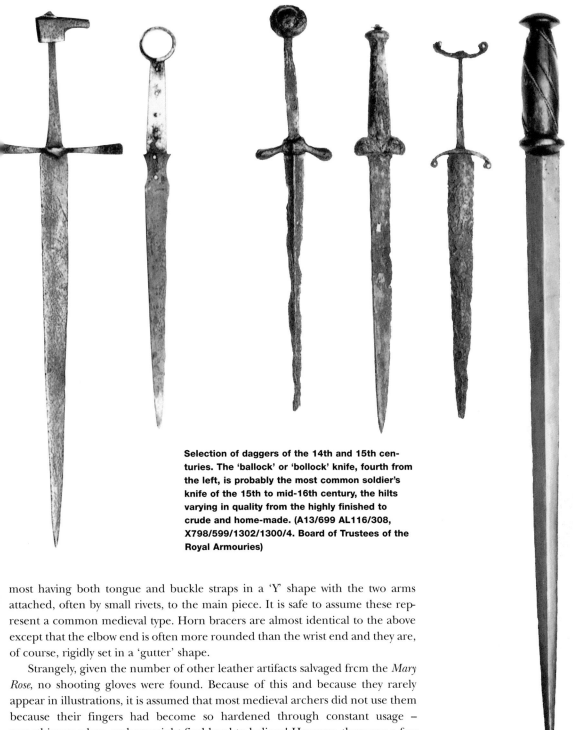

Selection of daggers of the 14th and 15th centuries. The 'ballock' or 'bollock' knife, fourth from the left, is probably the most common soldier's knife of the 15th to mid-16th century, the hilts varying in quality from the highly finished to crude and home-made. (A13/699 AL116/308, X798/599/1302/1300/4. Board of Trustees of the Royal Armouries)

most having both tongue and buckle straps in a 'Y' shape with the two arms attached, often by small rivets, to the main piece. It is safe to assume these represent a common medieval type. Horn bracers are almost identical to the above except that the elbow end is often more rounded than the wrist end and they are, of course, rigidly set in a 'gutter' shape.

Strangely, given the number of other leather artifacts salvaged from the *Mary Rose*, no shooting gloves were found. Because of this and because they rarely appear in illustrations, it is assumed that most medieval archers did not use them because their fingers had become so hardened through constant usage – something modern archers might find hard to believe! However, there are a few pictorial and written references, including one for John Howard's household archer, Daniel. Modern archers use either a 'full' glove, a 'skeleton' glove or a 'tab'. The full glove is, as its name implies, very similar to an ordinary glove but with the addition of extra leather pads sewn to the tips. To ensure a tight fit some also have loops that fit over the base of the fingers and are attached to thongs which are connected to a wrist strap. The full glove is the type almost always seen in medieval illustrations. The skeleton glove consists simply of pouches covering

The élite Scottish archer guard of Charles VII (shown here as one of the three Kings). A product of the strong Franco-Scottish alliance existing throughout the medieval period, they were formed in 1418 under the captainship of John Stewart of Darneley. The illustration is used to demonstrate the quality and uniformity of clothing and equipment of wealthy household archers. (*The Adoration of the Magi* by Jean Fouquet, from Les Heures d'Etienne Chevalier. Musée Condé, Chantilly. Photographie Giraudon)

the drawing fingers, often only from the tips to the second joint, and are likewise attached to thongs or thin straps connected to a wrist strap. The Zamorra Tapestry is, so far, the only known medieval illustration of anything resembling this type. The tab is just a flat piece of leather lying on the inside of the hand with either one or two holes into which the drawing fingers are let. There is no evidence at all for dating the tab before the end of the 18th century, surprising given its simplicity.

The back-quiver, so beloved of TV and film makers is categorically *never* seen in medieval illustrations. In fact, until the 16th century, quivers, as we understand the word, are never seen pictured on English archers. For carrying arrows the most common methods adopted by the English and most other north-west European archers were either to simply tuck them under their waist belt or to use what can best be described as 'arrow bags'. There are three basic recognisable types of bags. The first is simply the linen or canvas bag, of varying sizes, containing loose arrows and seen lying on the ground in the illustrations to Froissaart's Chronicles. The second is unique to the Schilling Chronicle illustrations showing archers in Charles the Bold's army of the 1470s and is described in the caption to one of those illustrations. The third, and most common, type appears as a tube of soft material, perhaps leather, canvas or linen, perhaps with a small rigid centre section, fastened at each end by a drawstring and attached, somehow, to the waistbelt. In action both ends were opened and folded back to expose the feathers and heads.

Shooting Technique

Obviously, the requirements of archery in medieval warfare were completely different to that needed by the modern recreational archer; consequently there are marked differences in stance and technique. For the English archers great emphasis was put on 'strong shooting' and long range – Henry VIII later made practice at long range compulsory – thereby encouraging the use of powerful bows, but the ability to shoot[11] such bows is not something that can be achieved easily. Medieval Englishmen were aware of this and emphasised the importance

---

11 An archer always 'shoots' or 'looses' his bow. The only time it is 'fired' is when someone puts a match to it.

of starting young (seven years was the traditional age for boys to begin their training) and 'growing up' with the bow, as Bishop Latimer's sermon to the young Edward VI in 1549: '... In my time my poor father was diligent to teach me to shoot as to learn any other thing, and so I think other men did teach their children. He taught me how to draw, how to lay my body in the bow and not to draw with the strength of my arms as other nations do, but with the strength of my body. I had my bows brought to me according to my age and strength and as I increase in them so my bows were made bigger, for men shall never shoot well except they be brought up in it.'

The most noticeable difference between the present-day archer and his ancestor is in the aiming method reflected by the point to which the arrow is 'drawn back'. There are four basic methods of aiming which can be categorised as follows: Purely instinctive; semi-instinctive; point-of-aim (POA); using a bowsight or mark on the bow.

Purely instinctive is how we throw stones and darts. The brain receives information from the eye, makes all the necessary calculations about weight and distance and passes this data to the arm. To be truly instinctive in archery the actual mechanics of shooting should be almost an unconscious act with all concentration centred on the eye – rather like changing gear when driving a car.

Semi-instinctive is as instinctive, above, but also to see the tip of the arrow in the periphery of vision and use it as a reference point.

The Duke of Burgundy entering a town led by trumpeters and archers of his guard wearing his livery. Note the waist quivers. (Flemish 1460-1480. British Library Royal MS E1 f12)

Arrows, unlike bullets, only fly in a straight line for very short distances and, like artillery shells, they actually travel in a parabolic curve. The POA archer establishes his 'point-blank' range, i.e. the distance at which, when sighting on the tip of the arrow, it flies to exactly where his eye is looking. For shorter and longer distances he does not aim at the target at all but at a point below or above it. Use of a sight, or mark, on the bow is self-explanatory but there is no evidence at all for their use in the medieval period.

Although Ascham does not detail aiming methods, he is clearly writing of POA when he describes archers who have '... invented some ways to espy a tree or a hill beyond the marks, or else have some notable thing betwixt the marks' and, perhaps, of semi-instinctive with '... others, and those very good archers, in drawing look at the mark until they come almost to the head, then they look at their shaft but, at the very loose, with a second sight, they find their mark again'. However, he disdains these methods as '... but shifts, and not to be followed in shooting straight. For having a mans' eye always on his mark is the only way to shoot straight' i.e. instinctively, which, he says, is '... so ready and easy a way, if it be learned in youth and confirmed with use, that a man shall never miss therein'.

Modern archers draw their arrows back to an 'anchor' point on their face or chin under the aiming eye. It is considered important to have this fixed reference point to ensure consistency of aim. While there are countless medieval illustrations depicting archers shooting with such a style, these are, as outlined in the Introduction, practically all of non-English origin. It is the author's belief that what distinguished the best English military archers from their contemporaries was their ability to shoot powerfully and accurately at both long and short ranges by drawing 'to the ear' and aiming instinctively. In fact, the phrase 'to the ear' is a generalisation and might be to any point between the ear and the breast (which is actually a natural 'locking' point for the shoulder). To lower the drawing hand is, in effect, to raise the bow hand, but it is a difficult technique with heavy bows. Ascham describes the difference between strong 'forehand archers' who could reach long distances while still being able to view the target over the bow hand, as compared to 'underhand archers' who had to elevate their bow arm and view the target *under* the bow hand to reach the same mark.

It is commonly assumed that drawing 'to the ear' automatically means shooting a very long arrow – up to 36 inches according to some writers – on the premise that modern archers only have a drawlength of 28-30 inches. This completely overlooks the practicalities of the method and the restrictions caused by the wearing of defensive apparel. Assuming a right-handed archer stands as a modern archer does and simply extends his draw from chin to ear, then the off-centre line of the arrow is greatly exaggerated and the arrow flies to the left. This angle is further increased if the archer is wearing a helmet, for then it is necessary for the drawing hand to be further away from the side of the head. To be able to shoot straight the archer has to bring his bow arm round to be in-line with his drawing hand which immediately shortens the draw-length. Another difference is in the position of the leading foot. Modern archers stand sideways-on with both feet at 90 degrees to the target. Medieval illustrations show the leading foot pointed towards the target. The effect of this is to bring the shoulder round and 'squarer-on' to the target thereby increasing the clearance of the string path from the chest, especially important if the archer is wearing padded clothing or a breastplate. It also contributes to the reduction in draw-length.

Also overlooked is the effect of compression on the human frame caused by shooting heavy bows. It was discovered during shooting sessions by Richard Galloway's group (average height 5' 10") that with heavy bows and the finger draw, the maximum draw-length by the strongest archers was 32 inches. Generally the draw-lengths were, depending on the height and strength of the archer, between 29 and 31 inches. It is therefore worth noting that the vast majority of war arrows, recovered from the *Mary Rose* are, reputedly, some 30½ inches long.

While a three-finger draw was certainly used and Ascham instructs on that style (though he was writing for the more genteel classes), the great majority of medieval illustrations show a two-finger hold. This gives a 'sharper' release as there is less friction on the string when loosed but its use is determined by strength. It was the origin of the Englishman's, still used, two finger 'salute', adopted by archers in the face of French threats to cut off the drawing fingers of any archer they captured.

TRAINING

It is usually stated that English soldiers of the medieval period received no military training and simply picked up their expertise from experience. It is therefore

The siege of Berwick. (The St. Albans Chronicle. Lambeth Palace Library MS 6 f174)

The battle of Agincourt. Following contemporary practice, the clothing and equipment depicted were the ones in fashion at the time of the painting. They illustrate the adoption by the English from the mid-15th century of the national livery jacket. Note the one archer's woollen hat, which, if worn, would have been over a metal skull cap. (The St. Albans Chronicle. Lambeth Palace Library MS 6 f243)

claimed that, because of this, after their exclusion from France in 1453, their 'battle-worthiness' decreased and a statement from the contemporary Burgundian chronicler, Philip de Commynes, about the 1475 army is often used to substantiate this: '… Yet these were not the Englishmen of his (i.e. Charles the Bold) father's day and the former wars with France. They were inexperienced and raw soldiers, ignorant of the French ways.' However, this overlooks the precedent of 1415 when, despite a 35-year absence from major campaigning the army of Harfleur and Agincourt did not perform too badly. It is also interesting to compare two other statements from the same chronicle. One earlier to the above when Commynes is remarking about Burgundian archers: '… Further, those who had never had a day's experience of their job are more valuable than those who are well trained, this is the opinion of the English who are the world's best archers.' This reflects a theory, still heard today, that it is better for officers to have recruits they are able to direct and mould to their own liking rather than veterans who usually have ways and opinions of their own. And in a later reference to the 1475 army, Commynes wrote: '… for if he [Charles the Bold] had ever wanted to use them it would have been necessary not to let them out of his sight for one full season in order to help them to train and instruct their army in our most important methods of warfare. When the English first come over no one is more stupid and clumsy but in a very short time they become very good, clever and brave soldiers'. Can we infer from this, particularly the phrase 'help them', that, once assembled, English soldiers did receive some form of training and instruction?

There would, of course, have been no need for any instruction in the shooting of the bow. Regardless of the statutes passed to encourage archery (including one lamenting that '… the kingdom, in short, becomes truly destitute of archers… '

written in 1363 – just seven years after Poitiers and 52 years before Agincourt) English archers were proud of their reputation and had plenty of practise through recreation and hunting and, after all, both retainers and levies were employed *because* of their skills. There was also no requirement to train them in any equivalent to the musketry 'firing by rank and file' for, though archers shot 'wholly together', it is not practical to expect them, especially with heavy bows, to draw, hold and loose them at exactly the same time and there is no evidence that they ever did so.

All fourteenth-century records are particularly reticent about any form of training for the ordinary soldier while the best 15th century example is the training ordered by Charles the Bold for his standing army where the archers were to practise working in conjunction with the pikemen. Amongst the many manoeuvres described, it was outlined how, during an advance, pikemen were to march in front of the archers and kneel on command so the latter could shoot over their heads. The archers were also to practise shooting while standing back to back or in other formations, always protected by pikemen. It is possible that Charles got the inspiration for many of the manoeuvres, as he did with most things connected with archery, from English precedents, though one needs to substitute pole-axe and bill for pike.

Breaking camp. A scene familiar to all armies, this one being Italian of the mid-15th century. Note the pack asses and the men rolling up the tent walls. Battens are clearly outlined in the material. ('An Army breaking camp' by Giovanni Bettini c. 1460. MS Canon. Class. Lat.81 f49v. Bodleian Library, Oxford)

There were various treatises written in medieval Europe recommending such things as how to conduct a siege but probably their closest equivalent to a full training manual was *De Rei Militari* written in the 4th century AD by Flavius Vegetius Renatus. This was reproduced fully or in paraphrase quite frequently from the second half of the 13th to the late 16th century – often translated into the vernacular. One English edition, *Knyghthode and Bataile*, was written in verse form in around 1458. Though sometimes making anachronistic references to the formations and make-up of the Roman legions, the fact that the text was continually modified to incorporate the latest military developments, and occasionally including comments on a current political situation, shows that this lengthy work was not simply regarded as a history. It recommends, for instance, how footmen should be taken out on route marches, in full kit, three times a month, how they should learn to march at a set pace to ensure good order – and suggests a speed of 20,000 paces in five hours (which works out approximately to $2\frac{1}{4}$ miles an hour). It commends running as good training and that all men, regardless of status, should be able to swim.

Just how far all this theory was ever applied in practice – and whether the levy were ever trained at all – we will probably never know but it is known that many commanders had this book in their library and it is not too fanciful to suggest that, for household and retained men in long-term employment, military training formed some part of their daily life.

Levied archers of Cheshire and Flint in the 1330's

A

Retained archers of the mid-14th to early 15th centuries

B

Battle of Agincourt, 1415

C

English archers assault French defences, Castillon 1453

D

Off duty archers practice their craft, c.1450-80

E

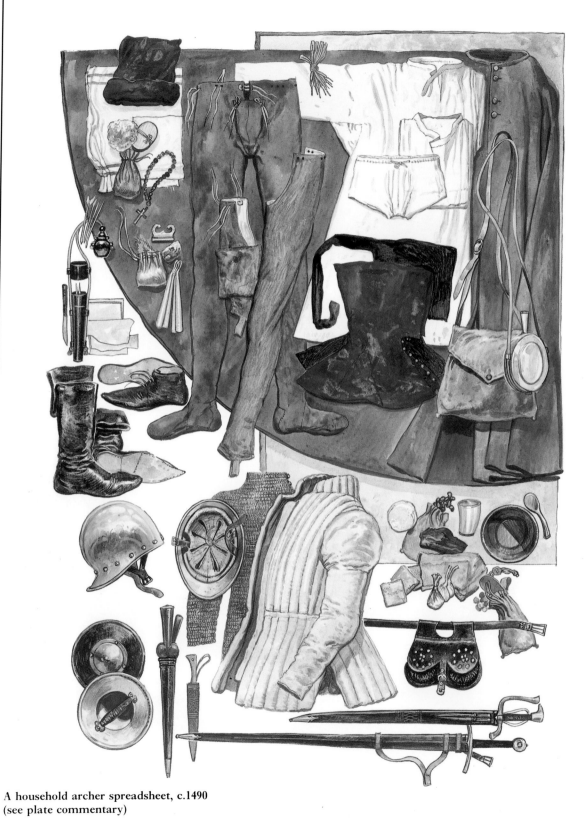

A household archer spreadsheet, c.1490
(see plate commentary)

F

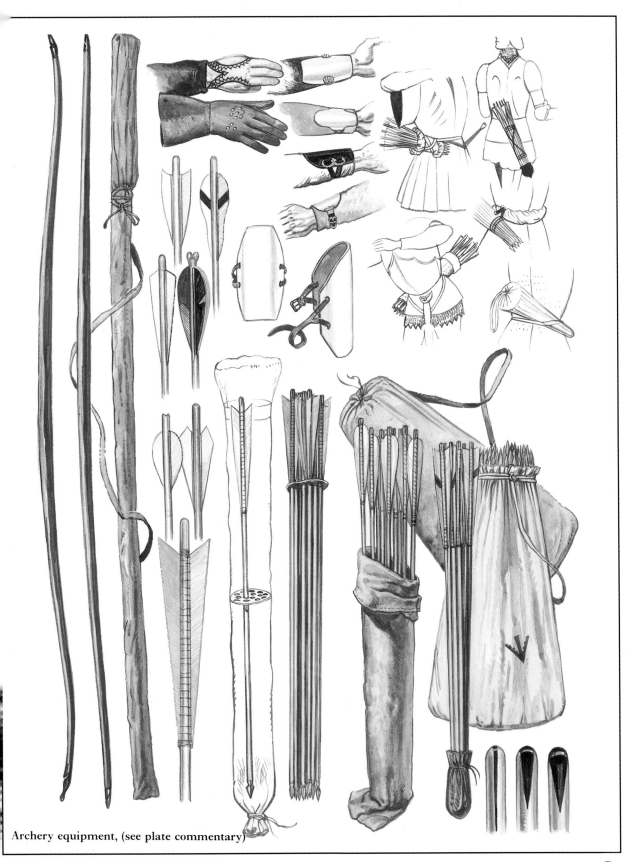

Archery equipment, (see plate commentary)

H   Bowyer discovered working after dark, Calais c. 1465

The tent of Antoine, Grand Bastard of Burgundy, 1475

I

J   Dying english archer, Burgundian campsite, 1475

Levied archers of York, 1482

K

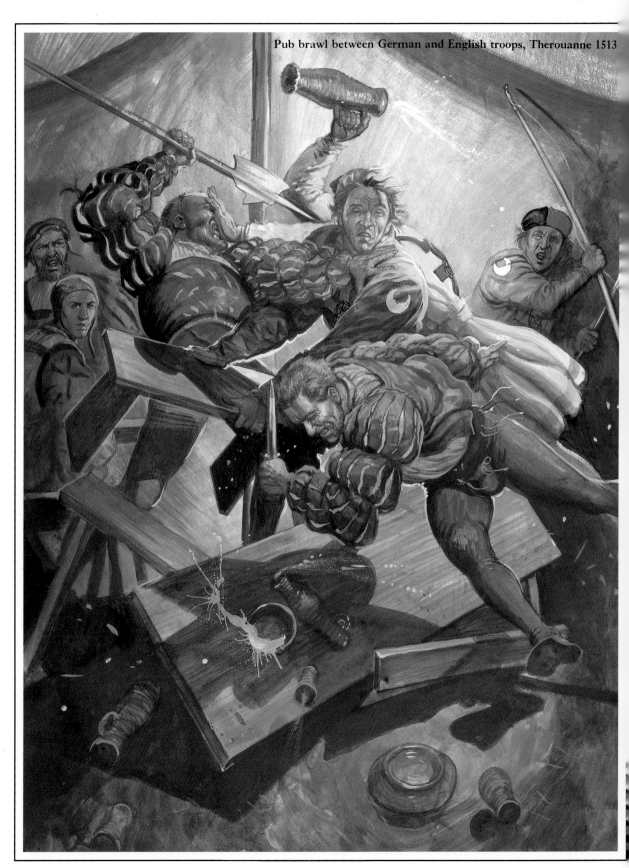

Pub brawl between German and English troops, Therouanne 1513

L

MOVEMENT AND TRANSPORT

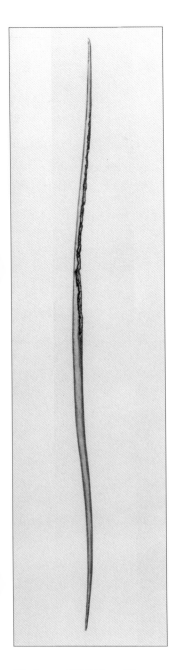

War bow c. 1545. One of the eight *Mary Rose* bows recovered by the Deane brothers in 1840. Watercolours were made of all the artefacts at the time of recovery but most of the items, including the bows, were sold at auction and, although the Royal Armouries has three, this one has long since disappeared. Note its reflex and recurve characteristics. (Courtesy of the City Museum and Art Gallery, Portsmouth)

The image of the English soldier fighting on foot has disguised the substantial number of horses present in their armies. It should be noted that, with the allowances for attendants and spares, an Earl usually took six horses, a knight-banneret five, a knight four, a man-at-arms three and a mounted archer one – though in 1361 Sir John Chandos allowed two horses for each mounted archer. The horses for household men and retainers were supplied or paid for by their employers and for the levy by their county or city. The York archers of 1481 received 2d a day towards their horse hire on top of their 6d a day wages.

The shipping of the horses overseas and back was paid for by the King. And when in 1352 the Earl of Stafford had to leave without his horses due to shortage of ships, the cost of purchasing remounts was also shouldered by the King. Compensation was paid for the loss of horses and because of this officials were appointed to make an inventory with brief description of the horses' colour and features.

Though it is generally understood that archers only rode to battle and then fought on foot, the author has seen four medieval illustrations of a 'longbow' being shot from horseback and knows of one recent occasion when a modern 'longbowman' shot from the back of a galloping horse.[12] A reference in Henry VII's regulations for the Stoke campaign in 1487 explains how mounted soldiers were '… at the furste sounde or blaste of the trumpet to saddil hys hors, at the 2d doo brydell, and at the 3d be redy on horsebake to wayte upon his highnesse, upon peyne of imprisonment'.

Though there are plenty of contemporary illustrations of water bottles and haversacks, there is not one showing a soldier in 'marching order'. It would seem the men put practically everything in wagons or on pack horses and each retained or levied contingent travelled as a sort of self-contained unit of personnel and equipment. The contemporary French chronicler Jean Le Bel records that for the 1359 invasion, Edward III's army contained 6,000 carts all brought over from England. Later he writes of '… 10,000 to 12,000 wagons with three good horses each brought from England' though whether as an increase to his previous estimate or different vehicles is not clear. The figures are no doubt exaggerated but the impression must have been of a vast number of wagons and carts. For the planned 1481 Scottish expedition Edward IV ordered that '… besides the Kynges carrage and provisicians, provisician be made for carrige of carts aboute Newcastell as shall move therine such of the Kings host as will by them and also other carts to the number of Vc [500] goyng after the host with vitaill'.

The size of these wagon parks was such that, in order to locate a particular wagon, some form of identification must have been necessary. Probably the system as recorded being used during the earlier Scottish campaigns of Edward I whereby each wagon carried a small flag or pennon bearing the 'owners' badge was still practised.

For the march from Harfleur to Calais, which led to the battle of Agincourt, when speed was of the essence, all the baggage was carried on pack horses and the heavy equipment and wagons left at Harfleur. The whole complex area of supply and management of large wagon trains, the necessary veterinary care for all the horse, picket lines, etc., has yet to be fully researched, but the wherewithal obviously existed and was well practiced.

The medieval English army was also capable of fast marches when necessary.

---

12 John Waller at the Tower of London in July 1993.

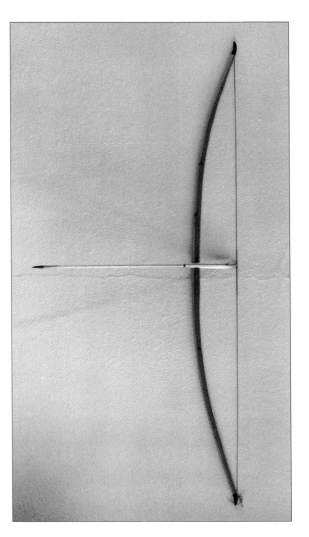

LEFT **Although Flemish, and ignoring the unfortunate distortion, this tapestry is an important reference which clearly shows the appearance of the typical war bow and arrow. The bow – and its diameter indicates a powerful one - has horn nocks at the tips and is without any handle binding. Note the diameter of the arrow, the length and height of the feathers and that they are tied down with thread. Detail from the 15th century 'History of Tarquin' now housed in the Zamora Cathedral Treasury, Spain. (Photo: Wim Swaan)**

BELOW **War bow c. 1993. Yew bow and aspen arrow made and photographed by Steve Jackson.**

For example, in the closing stages of the retreat to Tewkesbury in 1471 the Lancastrians travelled almost 50 miles in 36 hours while the pursuing Yorkists covered 36 miles in under 24 hours, even though both armies consisted primarily of footmen and were accompanied by artillery and some wagons.

Accommodation

Archers on campaign resided either in garrisons, billets or tents. We can tell from surviving records that household archers in England enjoyed a fair degree of comfort but there is no way of knowing how far these same standards applied to the garrisons, though castles were not, in general, the draughty, cold and cheerless places popular history makes them out to be.

Arranging soldiers' billets was one of the duties of the 'harbingers' who travelled ahead of the army and commandeered the rooms. Lodgings were allocated according to status and rules were laid down to prevent damage to the premises and the inhabitants. While these rules were usually enforced in England, the same niceties were not always observed in France. The same system was used in peacetime for the escorting soldiery of any lord or commander 'on tour'.

Harbingers were also responsible for finding suitable campsites. As usual, these needed to be on the high ground, dry and with water and wood available. In hostile areas the men fortified the camp. Even during Jack Cade's rebellion in 1450 the mob, which obviously included ex-soldiers, fortified their camp at Blackheath, outside London, '... dyked and staked well about, as it [have] been in the land of war'.

A great number of tents were normally transported though how far this was the aristocracy being greedy and how many were allocated to the common soldiers is not known. Tents were commonly made of canvas and constructed like modern ones with main poles and guy ropes. They came in all shapes and sizes – except square. Walls and roofs of the larger tents were sometimes braced with vertical timber batons sewn into sleeves in the canvas. These larger tents often had double walls for extra warmth and servants slept in the passageway in between. It is very likely that household archers and long term retainers were similarly allocated space in their employer's tent or were given tents of their own.

Soldiers not given tent space constructed 'hovels' which were simple shelters made of any available material – branches, foliage, straw, timber, etc. (exactly as seen in modern army manuals). Occasionally men went without any shelter, as on the night before Barnet in 1471 when they had to simply lie on the damp ground. Though lacking the ordered tent lines of later armies, the camp layout was regulated. Two main roadways, which were kept free of obstructions and guy ropes, dissected the camp into quarters and the commander's tent was usually placed at, or near, the crossroads. Near to his tent a large watch-fire was kept permanently alight and guarded and it was here that the sentries were advised of the night's passwords.

One of the most accurate paintings of medieval archery equipment. Note the shape of the bow being strung. However, despite the attention to detail, the postures of the archers is very stylised and the arrows are all on the 'wrong' side of the bow. (*Sebastian's altar* c. 1493 by the Master der Hi. Sippe. Wallraf Richartz Museum, Cologne)

It is not clear how many 'camp followers' accompanied the armies. The nature of much of the warfare may have restricted their presence. They are unlikely to have been with the mounted *chevauchees* of the14th century or in any great number with the very temporary armies of the Wars of the Roses. On the other hand, the breakdown in morale in France in the 1440s and 1450s may have given rise to a more 'laissez-faire' attitude. For the high quality armies of Henry V, of 1475 and 1513, measures were taken to ensure no camp followers or unnecessary servants were present.

A set of regulations drawn up by the Earl of Shrewsbury during the post-Agincourt campaigns dictates how if a man was found with a 'common woman' (i.e. a whore) in his lodging he was to lose a month's wages. Further, if anybody found such a woman, or group of them, in 'lodginge' he had permission to take any money found and to drive her out of camp and '… breke her arme'. On the return to England of the 1513 army, the Venetian observer, Nicolo di Favri, wrote '… They did not take wenches with them'. Commynes does not mention camp followers in 1475 but observed that the English, in addition to their soldiers, had '… others who both looked after all their tents, of which they had a great quantity, and attended their artillery and enclosed the camp. In the whole army there was not a single page… '.

MEDICAL SERVICES

Like many other aspects of medieval life, their knowledge of medicine has been underrated –though it was still primitive by modern standards. Anatomical dissection was practised in some European universities and there were numerous books, 'herbals', on plants and their medicinal values. Some of these herbals describe plants whose extracts could be used for anaesthetics. One 14th century source gives the recipe '... for to maken a drynke that men calle dwale to make a man slep-en whyles men kerve him' (i.e. perform surgery). Chaucer's Knight relates in his Tale how a gaoler was drugged by '... a certyn wyn with nercotikes and opie' (opium). Later in the same Tale the Knight describes how, in treating '... other wounds and to broken armes... ', some men '... hadden salves and some hadden charmes, fermancies of herbes'.

On the down side, much emphasis was placed on the 'contents' of the body and its' 'humours' and there was universal recognition that bleeding was needed as a palliative. And until Parre's revelations in the 16th century, serious wounds were often cauterised with hot pitch or similar unsuitable material.

There was no central medical department in the armies and it seems each contingent catered for its own needs, therefore a lot would have depended on the generosity and knowledge of the 'employer' whether city, county or individual. As with most other things, the household archer had the advantage. The King's Household was always accompanied by physicians and surgeons who signed Contracts of Indenture and came with their own small retinues of servants and archers. Henry Grosmont, first Duke of Lancaster, one of Edward III's principle commanders, even wrote a devotional treatise which included mention of ointments, plasters and 'fine, white bandages'. He describes how wounds must be dressed with clean bandages to hold the plaster and ointment in place and keep the dirt, dust and flies off. The Welsh in particular were regularly accompanied by doctors. In 1359 one Owen Charleton led a contingent of 1,120 men from North Wales which included 10 doctors. The York archers of 1482 were accompanied by a friar whose duties may well have included tending to their sick and wounded (some of the best medical care of the period was practised in the infirmaries of the religious houses).

At the last resort, and as throughout the ages, wounded men could rely on their comrades to assist them with any medical knowledge they might possess, putting them out of their misery if the wounds were untreatable. It is clear from the records that provision was made for garrison troops in the event of illness. They were still entitled to their daily pay (see 'Earnings') and as the commissioners were obliged to travel to them if they were not in the garrison, they must have been treated somewhere. Consideration was also given to prisoners. Froissart writes that, after the English defeat at Cocherel in 1364, every man '... took heed to his prisoners and dressing them that were hurt' – though the cynical might suggest this was because a live, ransomable, prisoner was worth considerably more

The four possible shapes for arrow shafts, exaggerated here for clarity. Technically and aerodynamically the most efficient shape is 'chested'. However, the best shape for war arrows is 'tapered', as it is easier for the narrowing shaft to follow through the hole made by the larger diameter head. (Drawing by Christa Hook)

HEAD

PARALLEL-SIDED

'TAPER-FASHION' or 'BOB-TAILED'

'BARRELLED'

'BIG BREASTED' or 'CHESTED'

NOCK

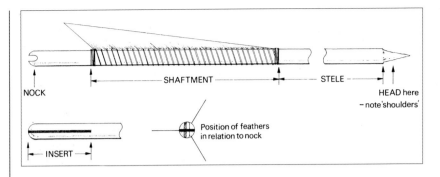

NOCK — SHAFTMENT — STELE — HEAD here – note 'shoulders'

Position of feathers in relation to nock

INSERT

than a dead one. But a more humane face of war is at least evident in the surrender conditions between the victorious French under the Count of Dunois and the defeated English under Matthew Gough at the siege of Bayeux in 1450 when '… all persons who are wounded or ill, being soldiers, may remain in the said town for one month in order that they may be cured and, if they wish to depart, their safe conduct shall be given them which shall be good and available for their journey into England'.

Wounds could be horrific but being predominantly of the cutting and stabbing type were at least straightforward and lacked the trauma associated with gunshot wounds of later centuries. Many men recovered from sword cuts, even if this removed all or part of a limb, and even stab wounds. There is a vivid description written by a German merchant in London in 1471 who witnessed the army marching out to Barnet field and saw them return: '… and many of their followers were wounded, mostly in the face or the lower half of the body, a very pitiable sight … those who had set out with good horses and sound bodies returned home with sorry nags and bandaged faces, some without noses etc. and preferred to stay indoors'.[13]

The great danger here is from complications such as peritonitis, which would inevitably have proved fatal – particularly when the arrowhead was left in the wound after the shaft had been removed. It was because of this that some Frenchmen thought the English poisoned their arrows.

The short, fast campaigns also kept the casualty rate low, certainly nothing like the horrific numbers of the l9th and 20th centuries. It is also true to say that in the majority of battles the English were the givers of death, not the receivers. Contemporary recordings of numbers must be treated with caution, but even allowing for exaggeration the casualties of the English at the major battles of Crecy, Poitiers, Agincourt, Verneuil and Flodden are surprisingly low – Agincourt miraculously so. Even during their defeat and eviction from France, the alacrity with which they surrendered resulted in few casualties. The exception was Castillon in 1453 which seems to have been a bloody battle, but the English army was relatively small. During the Wars of the Roses it was the policy of both sides, particularly of Edward IV, to 'spare the commons' to ensure public support. The exception here was Towton in 1461, probably the largest battle ever fought on British soil, which was long and hard and fought in appalling weather. (A ruder shock awaited those archers who volunteered to serve in Charles the Bolds army, for his enemy, the Swiss, took no prisoners and butchered all indiscriminately).

---

13 *'The Newsletter of Gerhard von Wessel 17th April 1471'* by John Adair, Journal of Army Historical Research, 1968. The locations of the wounds as described here are identical to those witnessed on the skeletons excavated from grave pits on the site of the battle of Wisby (1361), on the Swedish island of Gotland. The reference to bandaged faces is worthy of note – who supplied and applied them?

The great majority of *Mary Rose* shafts are reputedly of poplar, though other woods have been identified, and tapered from ½" diameter at the head to ⅜" at the nock. The socket for the heads, which, unfortunately, have all rusted away, would have fitted flush with the shaft. The drawlength from nock to shoulder is 30½" though a few vary 2" either side of that. All but two of the horn or bone inserts, which strengthen the nock against splitting from the thrust of the string, have disappeared but the slits cut in the shaft show they were 2" long and 1/16" thick, slightly tapering. The nock, or notch, for the string is ⅛" wide and ¼" deep. The feathers have also all rotted away but would certainly have been from the grey lag goose, though peacock wing and swan were sometimes used for 'best' arrows. Following the usual practise, the feathers were tied down with thread as well as glued – a couple of turns at each end and about five turns to the inch. The shaftment area has the remains of a greenish-tinted compound which was applied on top of the thread. Surviving marks show that the feathers on these shafts were 6"-6 ½" long, but there are fifteenth century references for feathers up to 12" long – whether different lengths related to different heads is not know. The height of the feathers can be deduced from the Zamora Tapestry. They start 2" down from the nock. The reason for this distance, much further than modern arrows, or even contemporary target ones, is that, probably to speed production, the feathers are simply cut to a triangular shape leaving the natural backward slope, so enough space has to be left to ensure the fingers of the drawing hand do not crush them.

A second type of arrow found, in much fewer numbers, was identical to the above in most respects except that the shafts were parallel sided, about 7/16" in diameter, and may have borne another type of head. (Drawing by Christa Hook)

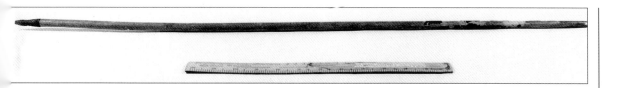

Though the average upper and middle class Englishman was personally more hygienic in the 14th and 15th centuries than he was to be in the following two, there is no reason to suppose his armies were any less vermin-ridden than any other in history and the greatest potential cause of death in an assembled army, especially during a siege, was disease and dysentery. The latter took a heavy toll of the English at Harfleur in 1415, despite the dangers being known. Shrewsbury's post-Agincourt campaign regulations ordered '… every lorde, capitaynes or governor of people do compell ther servnts and menye to berye ther careyn and bowelles abowte [i.e. away from] ther lodginges and within earth that no stynch be in ther lodginges wher through that any pestelence or mortalite myght fall within the oste, upon payne to make a mendes at the Kinges wille'.

The English were fortunate in that nearly all of their campaigns were of a short duration, particularly those of the 14th century *chevauchees* – which were also highly mobile. And, anyway, disease was the greatest killer in contemporary civilian life as well.

BELIEFS

Although the King was always accompanied by deans and chaplains, there is little evidence for organised church services for the whole army. As with most other things, religious needs were catered for within the contingents, and friars or chaplains almost always accompanied the retinues and levy. How devout the average soldier was is impossible to say. Medieval Englishmen maintained a healthy disrespect for the Pope and many of the bishops (England was still a Catholic country in this period) and the fact that military regulations were required to stop the pillage and robbing of churches and churchmen suggests that soldiers did not much respect the trappings of religion either. And murder and rape were not always restricted to secular members of the population.

The soldier would certainly have believed in God in his heaven and the Devil in hell and been concerned about his final destination. The friars would have performed the necessary daily services and conducted confessionals. Foreign observers remarked on the custom of English soldiers who, just before an attack, knelt, made the sign of the cross upon the ground and kissed it, taking a small piece of earth into their mouths – a symbol of man's mortality and eventual return to dust.

Soldiers also appear to have observed feast days and holy days. Jean Le Bel recounts in his chronicle of the 1359 campaign that some of the lords had brought with them '… severall small skiffs and small boats of leather so subtly made that they could easily hold three men for fishing on a lake or a river… so the lords and men of condition had fish during Lent but the commons made shift with what they might get'.

Superstitions still played a large part in men's lives and charms and good-luck tokens were carried to prevent or cure illness and protect the wearer against misfortune. At Flodden in 1513 the English commander, Thomas Howard, Earl

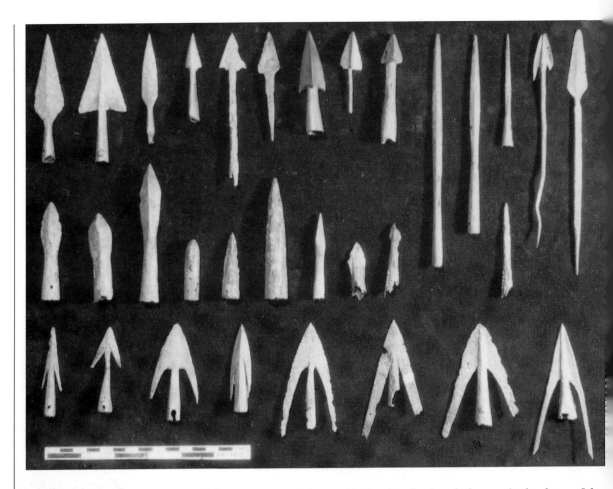

Examples of arrow and crossbow-bolt heads. Evidence suggests that, although not of an armour-piercing design, the one fourth from the left, bottom row, was the most common for war arrows. Note that some examples (hunting heads?) show a rivet hole in the socket, but it is highly unlikely this was done on war arrows (cf. the comment on 'fixing' in the text). (Courtesy of the Museum of London)

of Surrey, even carried a good-luck token for the whole army in the shape of the banner of St. Cuthbert which was reputed to contain a relic of the saint and to have been the same banner carried at the victorious battle of Neville's Cross in 1346. The best known example of superstition in the period is the effect that Joan of Arc was supposed to have had on the English soldiers during 1429-31. Known as the *Pucelle de Dieu*, she is credited with having caused the relief of the siege of Orleans, the English defeat at Patay and the fall in English fortunes. Many ordinary English soldiers were undoubtedly frightened of her and considered her capable of conjuring up supernatural powers. The Duke of Bedford, in a confidential report to the King and his council in 1434, claimed that everything had been going well in France until the relief of Orleans when '... the Pucelle that used fals enchantment and sorcerie' had '... not oonly lessened in greet partie the nombre of youre peuple there but aswel withdrawe the courage of the remenant'. But Joan's influence has been greatly exaggerated. Despite his report, Bedford had not considered it necessary to transmit or advertise the result of her trial or execution in 1431. There is no doubt that the Maid inspired the commanders and soldiers of the army she was with, but outside of that circle she was relatively unknown. The English chroniclers that do mention her make more of the fact she dressed 'as a man' and had the presumption to claim she was instructed by saints and angels. After her death they consign her to history as just another 'false witch', not unknown in medieval Europe. The decline in English fortunes at the time owed more to mismanagement from home and collapse in morale than it did to supernatural powers.

Behaviour

All soldiers were subject to the 'Statutes and Odinances of War', military regulations laid down or reaffirmed at the start of every campaign. The earliest extant full set are those issued by Richard II in 1386, but much would have been adopted from earlier codes. Henry V's 1415 regulations closely followed the 1386 set and, in turn, those of Edward IV and Henry VII follow their precedents. However, if the King was not accompanying the army, the statutes could be issued by the commander in his own name and might vary from their royal contemporary. It appears that, rather than the regulations being read out to the assembled army, copies were issued to contingent captains whose responsibility it was to ensure their men were familiar with them.

Punishments ranged from fines to death by hanging or beheading. Not surprisingly, the most severe punishments were ordained for crimes which might seriously endanger the safety of the army. In particular, any man who, during any action, cried 'Havoc' without due authority was to 'die therfor' – havoc being the signal that the enemy was decisively beaten and looting could begin. Any sentry

Liveried archers and cross-bowmen shooting into a besieged city. Women and children are bringing up refreshments for the men. Note the men recovering arrows shot out by the defenders. Of particular interest is the soldier wheeling the barrow with supplies of bundled arrows. (The siege of Jerusalem. *'Les Passages faits Outremer'*, c. 1490. Bibliothèque Nationale, Paris)

who deserted his watch without permission was to be beheaded and any man who set himself up as a captain and withdrew men from the army was to be hanged and the men that followed him beheaded. On the other hand, it is noticeable how lenient many of the punishments are and simple fines were common. The 1415 statutes are even more lenient than those of 1386 and also recognise that some soldiers might be innocently duped into an offence. For instance, in 1386 the originator and other 'beginners' of the cry 'havoc' were beheaded (and their bodies hung up by the arms as examples) but in 1415, while the originator was still executed, the others were just to be imprisoned '... till they have found surties [surety] that they shall no more offend'. Many of the statutes include the stipulation that horse and harness is to be confiscated until the offender has '... made fyne with the Constable and Marshall' (ie. paid a fine) and then his body is to be at 'the Kings will'. Some punishments reflect the status of the guilty party, for instance, in 1386 if any unauthorised person was '... to crie to horseback in the hoste for the great perill that might falle to all the host' then, if a man-at-arms or mounted archer, he was to lose his 'beste horse', but, '... if he be a archer on fote or other boye or page, he shall have the right ear cut off'. The removal of an ear is the only type of physical mutilation contained in any of the statutes. By 1415 the only time it is prescribed is for a groom or page who causes a serious disturbance through provoking an argument over 'armes, prisoners, lodging' or 'other thinge'. And, contrary to many people's impression of the medieval age, no statute demands punishment by, or with, torture.

There are no known descriptions of court-martials and perhaps a common archer did not warrant one, though a phrase in the 1415 statutes says if any man '... be juged to the death by the Kinge, Counstable, Marishall, or any other Juge ordynarye or any other office lawful... ', does not stipulate about the offenders status. The phrase 'the Kings will' seems also to have been valid even if the King did not accompany the army, so it would appear that punishments were not arbitrary and the accused got some form of hearing, even if only by correspondence.

It is unlikely we will ever discover just how many soldiers were executed but it is worth reflecting that Henry V's hanging of a soldier who stole from a church, a sacrilege and in direct contravention to one of the statutes, was an event notable enough for the chroniclers to record and Shakespeare to later make use of. Henry VIII, not famous for his kindliness, only had two soldiers, brothers, hanged during the 1513 expedition but another two involved, also brothers, went unpunished. In general, unruly behaviour or indiscipline, often caused either by the English soldiers' penchant for ale and wine or by long periods of enforced idleness through delays in embarkation, were effectively dealt with by the captains. Though on at least one occasion, the authority of even the most senior commanders was not enough. At the signing of the Treaty of Picquigny in 1475, Louis XI threw open the gates of Amiens to the English and provided unlimited quantities of free wine and food. Unsurprisingly, matters began to get out of hand and the worried French authorities appealed to

This archers' bracer is of cuir bouilli (hardened leather) and decorated with a crowned rose, acorns and oak leaves and the words 'ihc helpe' (Jesus help). The decoration was originally enhanced with gilding and colouring. Because of the rose & crown and the design of the wording the bracer has been dated to the early 16th century. Measurements (dimensions not exact) are: length 4¹⁵⁄₁₆" (125mm); width 5¹³⁄₁₆" (147mm); thickness of leather ⅛" (3mm).
It has been assumed that the fastening has always been by a thong passing through the holes. However, the holes do not completely 'pair', there being nine holes on one side and seven on the other all randomly place, and in most cases disfigure the decoration. During a close examination, kindly arranged by Dr. Gaimster of the British Museum, the author was able to establish that the original fastening had been by a tongue and buckle, or two tongues, on the end of 'Y' shaped straps riveted to the bracer – a common medieval method (and one which features on some of the surviving 'Mary Rose' bracers).
At some date, anywhere between the 16th and 19th centuries, through age or accident, the four original rivet holes, now enlarged and included with the others, had been ripped (the tears are just visible in the photograph, below the holes first and third left) and the method of fastening changed. (British Museum. Catalogue reference BM MLA 1922, 1 - 10, 1)

the English commanders to restore order. But the troops ignored their officers and only after the direct and personal intervention of the embarrassed Edward IV did the soldiers stagger back to camp.

All the statutes included clauses forbidding crimes against the civilian population; the 1415 ones even dictate death for anybody who burnt property without authorisation. Nevertheless, there were occasions when atrocities were committed and men, women and children killed without mercy – as at Limoges in 1370. Commanders tried to stem the worst excesses, Froissart records how, during the fighting at Caen in 1346, Sir Thomas Holland '... mounted again on his horse and rode into the streets and saved many lives of ladies, damsels and cloisterers from defoiling, for the soldiers were without mercy'. He also records that the next day Sir Geoffrey Harcourt '... with his banner rode from street to street and commanded in the Kings name none to be so hardy to put fire in any house, to slay any person nor to violate any woman'. But he also wrote '... there were done in that town many evil deeds, murders and robberies' for '... in a host such as the King of England was leading there must needs be some bad fellows and evildoers and men of little feeling'. When reading of the burning, plundering, rape and slaughter that took place in 14th century France two things should be taken into account. Firstly, the accepted laws of medieval warfare dictated that if a stronghold or town was called upon to surrender after its defences had become untenable but refused, thereby causing unnecessary casualties, then no mercy need be shown to the inhabitants. One chronicler claims this was the situation at Limoges. And Harcourt undertook his merciful actions at Caen after he had persuaded Edward III to revoke his command that all should be put to the sword and the town burned. Secondly, all these events took place against the background of the terrible desolation and destruction caused by the chevauchee – a policy ordained by the English King. In consequence, and in spite of the efforts and good governance by such men as Sir John Chandos, in areas where the English held sway the attitude of the local population could be extremely hostile. In an early example – and one that shows the committing of atrocities was not one way – following their recapture of Roche Derrien in 1347 a French chronicler recorded how the French army '... killed men and women without distinction of age and even babies suckling at the breast' (and these must have been local people!) after which the English garrison of 240 men were allowed to leave escorted by two Breton knights. But the two knights could do nothing when the people of a nearby town 'butchers, carpenters and others' came out and slaughtered the soldiers 'like sheep' and '... had the corpses carried away to quarries and great ditches outside the town where they were eaten by dogs and birds'. Things were better in the settled areas of post-Agincourt occupied France when Englishmen became intergrated into local society. But these men lost everything after French reconquest in 1450. A petition addressed to Henry VI in 1452 by 'churchmen, nobles, soldiers and others' requests payment of promised compensation for the property and goods they had had to abandon but a postscript adds '... this petition was neither conceded nor carried

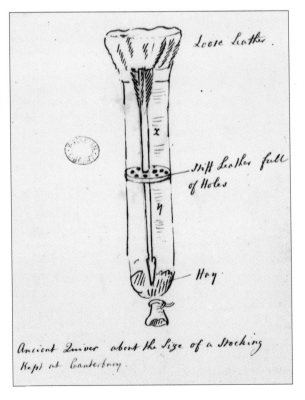

Several leather discs of about 5 in. diameter were recovered from the upper decks of the *Mary Rose*. The illustration dates from 1777 and comes from the notebook of the famous 18th-century antiquarian Francis Grose. (MS Top. Gen. e. 70. f24. The Bodleian Library, Oxford) The author is grateful to Mr. Graeme Rimer of the Royal Armouries for drawing his attention to this reference.

Loose Leather.

Stiff Leather full of Holes

Hay.

Ancient Quiver about the Size of a Stocking Kept at Canterbury.

An Italian reference from the late 15th century but included as it shows a rarely depicted guardroom scene. A woman is present and, while a game of backgammon is under way at one end of the table, a brawl has broken out at the other. ('Guard Room'. Anonymous, c. 1500. Castello di Issogne)

out. And because of this very many soldiers were reduced to the very greatest poverty, some, for grief, became ill and died, others were imprisoned for theft and were condemned to death by justice, while others still remained, as rebels, in the kingdom of France'.

It goes without saying that the endemic Anglo-Scottish border warfare could be equally as brutal as any in France but, apart from the saga of Berwick, there were no sustained occupations and actions generally consisted of tit-for-tat responses to incursions by one side or the other. The most serious battles between 1335 and 1513 were the result of English retaliation to French-prompted Scottish threats and invasions.

It is often suggested that the military reputation of the British soldier over the last three centuries owes much to strict, ingrained discipline and to the loyalty and esprit-de-corps generated by the Regimental system (plus a wish by the soldier 'not to let his mates down'). The archer had neither to subject himself to rigid drill, nor had he the benefits of the Regimental tradition, yet his armies were, in the main, surprisingly well ordered and obedient. And there always has to be something more than just a threat of punishment to make soldiers endure a winter siege of Calais in 1346-7, harsh winter campaigns in Scotland, that holds a dysentery-ridden army together on the march to, and at, Agincourt and inspires a band of archers to refuse to surrender and die to a man by the brook in the garden at Formigny in 1450. For the archer the 'X-factor' was probably threefold. Firstly, the loyalty given to a particular family or leader by the household soldier or retainer – especially with a charismatic leader such as John Talbot, Earl of Shrewsbury. Secondly, the loyalty and obedience given by the ordinary Englishman to the authority of the King. Thirdly, nationalism, bordering on xenophobia, that arose during the French wars – it was, for instance, during Edward III's reign that English replaced French as the language of the court.

Perhaps the best description we have of English archers is from a Spanish chronicle from the end of the 15th century, especially important as it was written

Liveried Burgundian archers of Charles the Bold. Their style of shooting, with its high, short draw, is one instantly recognisable to modern archers. (Bern Historical Museum)

by an impartial foreign observer. It is valuable because it illustrates the attitude of the English soldier and his behaviour in battle and proves the exceptions to the normally accepted ratio of men-at-arms to archers and the way of fighting.[14] In 1486 Sir Edward Woodville took a retinue of 200 men-at-arms and 100 archers to Spain to help fight the Moors in the conquest of Granada. Friar Antonio Agapida, when writing his *Chronicle of the Conquest of Granada* described the Englishmen thus: 'This cavalier was from the island of England and brought with him a train of his vassals, men who had been hardened in certain civil wars which had raged in their country. They were a comely race of men but too fair and fresh for [the appearance] of warriors. They were huge feeders also and deep carousers and could not accommodate themselves to the sober diet of our troops, but must fain eat and drink after the manner of their own country. They were often noisy and unruly, also, in their wassail, and their quarter of the camp was prone to be a scene of loud revel and sudden brawl. They were withal of great pride, yet it was not like our inflammable Spanish pride... their pride was silent and contumelious. Though from a remote and somewhat barbarous island, they yet believed them-selves the most perfect men on earth... With all this, it must be said of them that they were marvellous good men in the field, dexterous archers and powerful with the battle axe. In their great pride and self will, they always sought to press in their advantage and take the post of danger... They did not rush forward fiercely, or make a brilliant onset, like the Moorish and Spanish troops but went into the fight deliberately, and persisted obstinately and were slow to find out when they were beaten'.

And later, in recording an action during the siege of the Moorish city of Loja, the friar continued: 'He [i.e. Woodville] was followed by a body of his yeomen armed in a like manner [that is, with swords and battle axes] and by a band of archers with bows made of the tough English yew tree.[15] The earl turned to his troops and addressed them bluntly according to the manner of the country. "Remember my merry men all" he said, "the eyes of strangers are upon you. You are in a foreign land, fighting for the glory of God and the honour of Merry Old England!" A loud shout was the reply. The earl waved his battle axe over his head.

---

14 What follows is taken almost verbatim from the booklet: *'The Battle of Bosworth'* by Dr. Williams.
15 The bows were unlikely to have been of English yew, but an understandable mistake by the friar.

The archer on land. A detail from a battle scene in the Beauchamp Pageant. This manuscript, dating from the 1480s-90s, contains superb detailed drawings of clothing, armour and equipment of the period. Note that the foreground archer wears, over his mail shirt, a brigandine or plated jack with large single rivets. Note also the sheaf of arrows held at the waist. (British Library Cotton MS Julius E IV f20v)

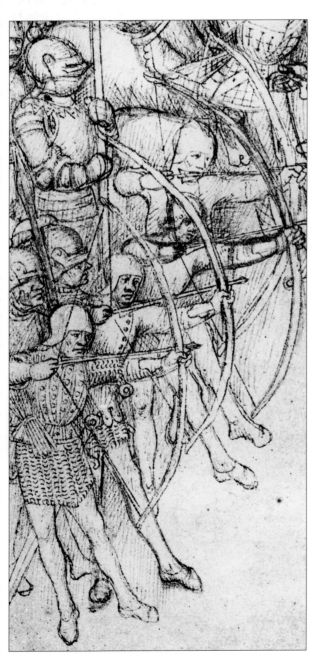

"St. George for England" he cried. They soon made their way into the midst of the enemy but when engaged in the hottest of the fight they made no shouts or outcries. They pressed steadily forward dealing blows right and left, hewing down Moors, and cutting their way with their battle axes like woodmen in the forest, while the archers, pressing into the opening they made, plied their bows vigorously and spread death on every side'.

BIBLIOGRAPHY

The Newsletter of Gerhard von Wessel 17th April 1471 by John Adair. Journal of Army Historical Research 1968

Rev. J. Stevenson (ed), *Letters and Papers illustrative of the Wars of the English in France* (2 vols. London 1861, 1864)

Rev. J. Stevenson (ed), *Narratives of the Expulsion of the English from Normandy 1449-50* (Rolls Series. London 1863)

G.C. Macauley (ed), *The Chronicles of Froissart.* Translated by John Berners *c.* 1523 (London 1895)

Sir H. Nicolas, *History of the Battle of Agincourt* (3rd Edition, Thomson Press, India, Ltd. 1833. Reprinted by H. Pordes, London 1971). This is still the most comprehensive history of the battle. Contains many informative appendices and transcripts of all the known contemporary accounts.

Roger Ascham, *'Toxophilus' 1545.* (Reprinted by the Simon Archery Foundation, Manchester 1985)

H.J. Hewitt, *The Organisation of War under Edward III 1338-62* (Manchester University Press 1966). This is an excellent and valuable book. Highly recommended to anyone with an interest in fourteenth-century English military history.

Michael Powicke, *Military Obligation in Medieval England* (Clarendon Press, Oxford, 1962). Contains much useful information but a difficult read and in dire need of a glossary and an enlarged index.

Kenneth Fowler, *The Age of Plantagenet and Valois* (Elek Books Ltd. London 1967). The best general history of the Hundred Years War.

Michael Jones (trans), *Philippe de Commynes Memoirs* (Penguin Classics 1972)

THE PLATES

A: LEVIED ARCHERS OF CHESHIRE AND FLINT IN THE 1330S

One wears a coat over his livery and has a second pair of single-leg hose over the first for extra warmth. The bows, swords and bucklers are their own, but, as well as the livery, they have been issued with arrows – though no defensive wear.

B: RETAINED ARCHERS OF THE MID-14TH TO EARLY 15TH CENTURY

The quality of their equipment denotes household men and most of it would have been issued to them. Both are wearing bascinet helmets, fitted with mail aventails, and padded gambesons.

The left-hand figure has the aventail secured to the gambeson by 'arming points'. The right-hand figure, a mounted archer, has leg armour. Both have the English national sign of the red St. George's cross stitched to the gambesons. They demonstrate the two medieval methods of 'stringing' the bows, the one on the right depicted more often. Nearly all modern representations of archers show another technique. That of placing a leg between the bow and string, resting the lower bow tip on the instep of the other foot and 'bending' the bow around the back of the thigh.This is a style born through not having the strength for the above two methods, is bad for the bow and has yet to be seen in a medieval illustration (and, yes, the author has been guilty of it).

C: AGINCOURT

The foreground archer in the act of drawing to the ear – all attention centred on his intended target. The loosened hosen was probably a necessity owing to the varying degrees of dysentery with which many of the men were afflicted. The chroniclers do not tell us how the stakes were arranged. It would have been more effective, and easier to place, for them to have been staggered to give defence in depth with the archers in amongst them – and it should be remembered that the men were moved forward from their original position and the stakes had to be relocated. On the other hand, the English were greatly outnumbered and the length of the line may have meant they were spread thinly.

D: CASTILLON, 1453

The French invaded and captured Aquitaine in 1451. The English put together a small army in 1452 under the leadership of John Talbot, Earl of Shrewsbury, which, when it landed, caused the French garrisons to flee.

Charles VII then sent, in 1453, an army back again. This was too powerful for Talbot to take on, but when the French commander split his forces with one division, under the command of Jean Bureau, besieging Castillon, Talbot decided to attack it. Bureau had had constructed a ditched, palisaded enclosure, strongly fortified with artillery. Unfortunately, English scouts wrongly identified it as a simple camp and, when a large dust cloud was thrown up when the French relocated their horses, wrongly assumed they were retiring. Acting on this news, Talbot set off in 'pursuit' with the mounted element of his army, leaving the footmen to follow on. On discovering his mistake, and despite strong objections from his senior commanders, Talbot nevertheless decided on immediate attack.

The English were held by the defences and mown down by artillery fire. Talbot, traditionally in civilian clothes and mounted on a small white pony (having sworn an oath when captured some years previously never to bear arms against the French again), was wounded and his pony killed by a culverin shot while on the earthworks. A French soldier then jumped down, crossed the ditch and killed him while he lay pinned by his pony's body. A sally by French mounted men-at-arms finally broke the English. The retreating English met the advancing footmen, who immediately retired back to Bordeaux, which surrendered after two days. Castillon was one of England's most significant defeats and, despite later optimistic plans, the end of her ambitions in France.

Our picture shows the dismounted archers during their futile assult on the French position. They wear the English national livery jacket, with Talbot's badge of a hunting dog (the Talbot), over various types of defensive wear.

E: CASTLE [ANYWHERE], C. 1450-80

Off-duty archers, one accompanied by his son, indulging in friendly, informal recreational competition, watched by a soldier about to go on duty. The archer sitting with a girl, perhaps his wife or perhaps just another employee of the castle staff, is shirtless but wears a pourpoint to hold his hose in place. The other archers have kept their livery coats on. The hose is all of a uniform colour and part of the livery issue. The target is a simple board on a pole, a typical target even for very long distances.

Archery competitions were very common and wagers usually placed – employers often taking a keen interest, both professionally and financially.

The archer at sea. The archer on the right is clearly drawing 'to the ear'. (British Library, Cotton MS Julius E IV f18v)

F: A HOUSEHOLD ARCHER'S SPREADSHEET FROM THE LATTER HALF OF OUR PERIOD

Clothing and equipment ready for wearing or packing for campaign service. Included are a travelling cloak and hoods, washing items (note the sponge), candles and a flint & steel, money, eating utensils with some 'emergency rations' and a canteen and haversack – the latter referred to in a Paston letter of 1492 as a 'gardyvyan'. This man was probably a junior officer as he can obviously read and write and carries parchment, a travelling set of ink pot and quill-pen container, spare quills and a 'pen-knife'.

G: ARCHERY EQUIPMENT

A recurved and a straight-limbed bow, the latter beginning to follow the string. Various shapes of feathers seen on target arrows, some completely or partially dyed. Note the bulbous nock of the arrow with red and black feathers, this was probably done to strengthen this area and as an alternative to inserting a strip of harder material (cf., for example, the Luttrell Psalter illustration). The 'full' and 'skeleton' shooting glove, various bracers, the one on its own with the brown leather strap a copy of one found on the Mary Rose. Differing arrangements of the waist quivers with, below, examples of arrow bags. The feathers of the war arrow are all tied down but only one set shows the green (because it is mixed with verdigris) gluing compound. Some medieval illustrations show this area red and some plain. So either some other medium was used with the glue or, perhaps, just the glue on its own, though this is unlikely. The practice of first gluing the feathers on, tying them down and then applying a thick compound over the thread and base of the feathers was a long-lived one. The Saxons had done it, using pitch.

At bottom right are shown half-, three-quarter and full nocks. The first used on war arrows, the other two, though not common, on 'best' target arrows.

H: CALAIS, C. 1465

The 'Scout Watch' discover a bowyer working at night. To ensure product quality various laws were passed throughout the period to ensure bowyers did not do this – craftsmen not having the advantage of modern artificial light.

Bows in varying stages of completion fill the workshop, some already fitted with the horn nocks brought in from outside suppliers and ready for the strings, stacked in coils. The bowyer holds a small 'flote' (float), a tool consisting of a series of blades set in a wooden handle. Because we have no actual example of a woodworker's bench or vice (though there are some of metalworkers, i.e. armourers), the one depicted is conjectural, though based on known working practices. The archers, armed with pole and side arms, are wearing livery coats in the colour, and with the badge, of

The archer in foreign service. English archers of Charles the Bold's army. This Chronicle consistently identifies these archers as wearing distinctive short jacks with high collars. (*Chronicle of Diebold Schilling*. Bibliothèque de la Bourgeoisie de Berne)

Warwick the 'Kingmaker', a popular Captain of Calais from 1455 to 1471. The relationship between the permanent soldiers of Calais paid for by the town and thoses brought in by an appointed Captain is not yet fully understood, but these archers represent Warwick's household men.

Watches were divided in both garrisons and armies into the 'Stand Watch', stationary guards, 'Scout Watch', those on patrol, and the 'Search Watch', who policed the others.

I: BURGUNDIAN CAMPSITE, 1475 (1)

Hand-picked archers of the guard of Antoine, Grand Bastard of Burgundy, a commander of Charles the Bold's army, and one of his messengers. Antoine's badge of a 'barbican', the castle defence equivalent of a ship's gunport, is visible on the messenger's doublet. The scene is set inside Antoine's tent, which is fitted out to a luxurious degree – a richly woven tapestry is on the wall behind two waiting attendants.

English archers were second in numbers to the Italians as foreign servicemen in Charles the Bold's armies and, from their first major action at the siege of Nijmegen in 1473, where they distinguished themselves, they remained a trusted and important component. In 1476 there were 780 mounted archers in the Duke's household guard. Unfortunately, they therefore suffered the consequences and very few returned home to England after Charles's defeat and death at Nancy in 1477.

J: BURGUNDIAN CAMPSITE, 1475 (2)

The same location as above, but the other end of the scale. Antoine's tent is visible in the background, in the foreground an archer, dying of illness far from home, lies on a mattress in a hovel attended by a friar, a camp follower and a friend. Other hovels of straw and timber are behind his simple shelter of canvas.

The standing archer wears a travelling garment known as a 'huke' and carries a straw hat. Another such hat rests on the tools in the right foreground. Straw hats were produced in their thousands and worn by all classes of men. On this man's upper sleeve is stitched the red St. Andrew's cross, the identifying sign for all Charles's soldiers.

In the middle distance, archers and pikemen can be seen practising one of the tactical formations laid down in Charles's Ordinances.

K: LEVIED ARCHERS OF YORK, 1482

The levied archers of York on their way to join the main army

A dead archer from the Schilling Chronicle. This view of the arrow bag shows the heads protruding from the opening. In all the illustrations the bags retain their shape, indicating that they had an internal framework – perhaps of wicker. (Bibliothèque de la Bourgeoisie de Berne)

RIGHT A rare illustration of a company of mounted archers. These are wearing liveried brigandines of blue and red. Of great importance is the view of the closed waist quivers clearly showing the drawcord fastening arrangement. (*Les Passages faits Outremer*. Bibliothèque Nationale, Paris)

A 15th-century army on the march against a background of ruined townships and castles. The two-wheeled cart, drawn by one horse, and the four-wheeled cart, drawn by three horses, were used in their hundreds throughout the medieval period. (Chronique de Hainaut. Bibliothèque Royale Albert 1er, Brussels)

for the campaign in Scotland. The men left York, after a minor mutiny, in July. There were 100 of them, all mounted, led by two captains, John Brackenbury and Thomas Davyson (who each had a servant), and accompanied by a standard bearer and a friar. They had one, or perhaps two, carts as two carters also travelled. The men are depicted wearing the national livery jacket, as all the army was ordered to do, though some are also wearing or carrying a coat – as one of the carters is. They were entitled to wear the livery badge of their city, but the badge shown here is conjectural (taken from York's coat of arms) as the actual one is not recorded.

These men should have been at the siege of Berwick, the occupation of Edinburgh or the battle of Hatton Field, which, contrary to earlier belief, may have been a major action.

L: FRANCE, DISTURBANCES, 1513

A brawl has erupted in a beer tent between English archers and their German 'allies' during the campaigning before Thérouanne. Disturbances such as this were not unknown during the campaign, owing to the Germans' refusal to take orders from any but their own officers – despite

instructions to the contrary from the Emperor Maximilian. The most severe incident happened on 15 August, when numbers of English and Germans fought each other, resulting in fatalities. At one point German gunners trained their artillery on the English, and German pikemen and English archers actually confronted each other.

Maximilian, who was a witness to the event, was impressed by the way the English officers were able to restore order amongst their men. This indicates a high level of discipline.

However, despite the occasional disturbance, the army of 1513 was the finest one to leave England during the 16th century.

LEFT **An early war memorial. Among the stained-glass windows installed during his enlargement of the church at Middleton, near Manchester, Sir Ralph Assheton included one commemorating sixteen of his archers who had fought for him at Flodden. All are dressed in blue livery coats and each carries a yew bow and a sheaf of war arrows. Their names are inscribed alongside their bows. (Courtesy of the Parochial Parish Council of St. Leonards and the Reverend Nicholas Feist)**

ABOVE **The meeting of Henry VII of England and Philip of Spain from an engraving by Hans Burgkmeir, dated 1516, in the fictionalised autobiography of the Emperor Maximilian. The archers of the King's guard are in full armour and carrying tall, reflexed bows. (From a reprint of *'Der Weisskunig'* published in Vienna in 1891. Board of Trustees of the Royal Armouries)**

INDEX

(References to illustrations are shown in **bold**. Plates are shown with caption locators in brackets.)